TABLE OF CONTENTS

Top 20 Test Taking Tips

1. Carefully follow all the test registration procedures
2. Know the test directions, duration, topics, question types, how many questions
3. Setup a flexible study schedule at least 3-4 weeks before test day
4. Study during the time of day you are most alert, relaxed, and stress free
5. Maximize your learning style; visual learner use visual study aids, auditory learner use auditory study aids
6. Focus on your weakest knowledge base
7. Find a study partner to review with and help clarify questions
8. Practice, practice, practice
9. Get a good night's sleep; don't try to cram the night before the test
10. Eat a well balanced meal
11. Know the exact physical location of the testing site; drive the route to the site prior to test day
12. Bring a set of ear plugs; the testing center could be noisy
13. Wear comfortable, loose fitting, layered clothing to the testing center; prepare for it to be either cold or hot during the test
14. Bring at least 2 current forms of ID to the testing center
15. Arrive to the test early; be prepared to wait and be patient
16. Eliminate the obviously wrong answer choices, then guess the first remaining choice
17. Pace yourself; don't rush, but keep working and move on if you get stuck
18. Maintain a positive attitude even if the test is going poorly
19. Keep your first answer unless you are positive it is wrong
20. Check your work, don't make a careless mistake

Foundations of Professional Organizing

Characteristics of a professional organizer

A professional organizer is someone who helps people, families, and businesses make their living and working places simpler and more efficient. A professional organizer meets with clients and performs an initial assessment, after which the organizer creates an action plan. This plan can be purely physical in nature, or it can include a mixture of physical, mental, and behavioral activities. Professional organizers can help clients manage their time and resources better. They can improve the client's efficiency in almost every area of his or her life. To accomplish this, however, the professional organizer must call upon not only his or her training, but his or her empathy and creativity. Organizing may sound pragmatic, but it can be a deeply emotional process for many clients. Often, organization problems are symptomatic of other issues in the client's life. A professional organizer should not overstep the limitations of his or her training, but should nevertheless be aware that his or her work is integral in the life of the client.

Characteristics of the effectively organized environment

It is a myth of professional organizing that all completed projects will look the same. There are some common tricks and techniques to professional organization, but it is more important to identify the qualities and needs of the client and to reflect these in the completed environment. A professional organizer should always approach projects from the perspective of the client; the goal should be to give the client what he or she wants, not what the organizer would want in his or her own life. An ideal environment will enable the client to feel more alive and less like a prisoner of his or her possessions and disorganization. A professional organizer must develop a comprehensive and detailed knowledge of the client's habits in order to create the proper environment.

Approaches to self-selection as a professional organizer

Many people want to be organized, and many people feel they are organized, but only a few people are truly gifted in this area. Professional organization is a vocation, and while it is possible to develop the skills to succeed in the field, the innate drive to organize cannot be learned. Before becoming a professional organizer, a person should consider the role that organization has played in his or her life. A successful professional organizer is usually someone who has always felt compelled to make both living and working spaces as efficient as possible. A professional organizer may have read books and subscribed to magazines on home improvement and organization. Many professional organizers have undertaken projects on their own in the past, whether for themselves or for family and friends. There are some careers, like teacher, nurse, and administrative assistant that seem linked to organization. Many people move from one of these careers into professional organization. Before setting out on this path, though, a person should also consider the type of organizing to which they feel drawn. Professional organizers may specialize in event coordination, time management, and home improvement, just to name a few.

Specializations

Professional organizers may take on a range of projects, or they may develop a specialization. For instance, many professional organizers focus on home improvements. Even among these, there are organizers who work exclusively with kitchens, bedrooms, or storage spaces, like garages and basements. Other professional organizers focus on clutter and collections, like photographs and other memorabilia. For some professional organizers, the passion is paper: these specialists focus their work on eliminating piles of bills, notes, books, magazines, and newspapers. Organizers may also help clients plan how new spaces will be used. For instance, when a business moves into new office space, it will often hire a professional organizer to create the floor plan. Some professional organizers work on time management and don't deal with physical constraints at all. Some organizers help people and businesses develop filing systems.

Types of clients

A professional organizer is likely to work with a variety of clients, though some pros will settle into a specialty customer base. At first, it is usually a good idea to see a range of clients, both to explore different types of work and to gain experience dealing with different types of client. Professional organizers may work with individuals, families, and businesses. Some pros focus on working with people with special needs, like the disabled or the elderly. Some pros spend most of their time with students, while others specialize on working with the heads of households. Some professional organizers work mainly with the owners of small, home-based businesses. Professional organizers should be aware that different clients will have different needs. The skills required to succeed with one type of

client may be quite different than those needed to satisfy another.

Ways a client's learning style can contribute to disorganization

Learning style can play a significant role in the degree and characteristics of a client's disorganization. For instance, clients who are primarily visual learners tend to amass piles of unread books, magazines, and other papers. These clients have an innate tendency to engage with the world through text, and so it can be very difficult for them to discard materials which they believe may be of some interest in the future. There are also ways in which the client's learning style can be used to formulate the organization plan. For example, tactile learners need to get physically involved with a project, while visual learners need to see progress. Clients who learn best with their ears need constant encouragement and explanation from the organizer. It is important for the organizer to gain an understanding of the client's learning style at the beginning of the project and use this information to improve the quality of service.

Physical health and cultural factors can contribute to disorganization

When a client suffers from a physical illness or injury, he or she is more likely to struggle with disorganization. Paradoxically, clients whose physical infirmity prevents them from using many of their possessions tend to accumulate more. Sometimes, a client will be physically unable to remove the unwanted objects from his or her house. A professional organizer must be sensitive to the physical health issues that cause disorganization. A client's cultural background may have some influence on his or her organization problems, as well. For instance, in some cultures it is considered immoral to throw away usable items. A professional organizer should emphasize charitable donation to such clients. The professional organizer should always be aware of how cultural factors are influencing disorganization, and should never make any remarks or suggest any projects that risk offending the client.

How age and gender can influence organization problems

As a person grows older, he or she is more likely to accumulate bad organization habits and unnecessary possessions. For instance, elderly people are often confused about the health and medical paperwork that needs to be retained. Establishing a good system for managing financial and personal papers is a common emphasis when working with senior citizens. Younger clients tend to have more problems with excessive amounts of clothing and entertainment equipment. A client's gender may also influence his or her disorganization profile. Women are more likely to have organization problems in the bathroom and the bedroom closet, while male clients tend to need more help in the garage or the basement. Of course, these are broad generalizations, and a professional organizer should avoid making gender-based assumptions during the assessment and planning phases of a project. It is better to treat each new client as a special case.

Costs of starting a professional organizing business

Initiating a business as a professional organizer is not as expensive as one might think. However, there are a number of things that every organizer must acquire before beginning operations. Whether working from an office or one's home, a professional organizer must possess some basic office supplies and equipment. A professional organizer also needs to pay

for advertising and marketing. Perhaps the main financial obstacle to beginning as a professional organizer, however, is leaving behind whatever source of income one had in the past. Most people who become professional organizers are arriving from a different field of employment, and it can take a while to build a sustainable list of clients. It is a good idea to have some savings set aside before becoming a professional organizer.

Four basic steps of every organization project

Organization projects come in all forms, which can be overwhelming for the beginning professional. There is a temptation to treat each client and project as entirely new and unique, which shows admirable respect to the client, but can result in the organizer being somewhat lost. It is best to have a simple, concrete process to apply to every new project. Even within established forms, there is plenty of room for creativity. For a professional organizer, there are four basic steps to every project: assess, plan, implement, and evaluate. If a professional organizer uses this four-step approach, he or she can maintain control of new projects. Some professional organizers want to rush to the implementation stage, but this can be avoided by paying respect to the four-step process.

Value of Internet marketing

The Internet has massively expanded marketing possibilities for professional organizers. Indeed, some organizers do all of their marketing online. For a low cost, an organizer can arrange for his or her name to appear among local search results for organizing services. There are many search engine optimization tricks a professional organizer can use to make sure potential clients find them. Some organizers hire web experts to drive traffic to their websites. Another great tool for professional organizers is social media. Professional organizers can establish business accounts on Facebook and Twitter, where they can keep clients and potential clients informed about package deals and new services. Many organizers regularly post organizing tips to their social media accounts, just to give interested parties a taste of the services they can provide. Organizers who really like to write might consider keeping a blog about their professional lives.

Obtaining business through personal connections

Especially at first, a professional organizer will obtain much of his or her business through personal connections. Most professionals get their start by providing discounted services to family and friends. Others gain a foothold in the industry by serving as an apprentice for an established professional. In either case, the aspiring professional organizer needs to cultivate these personal connections so as to generate more business. The organizer should tell his or her family and friends to spread the word about the new business. When meeting with colleagues, the organizer should explicitly state that he or she is looking for new clients. If an organizer can cultivate a good relationship with a professional who is already working in the field, it can create a mutually beneficial arrangement in which each professional refers clients to the other. This can be a great way to keep clients happy and maintain steady business.

Marketing

In restaurants
One unusual place where professional organizers can market themselves is in restaurants. The people who solicit the services of professional organizers are often affluent and likely to eat out frequently. Many restaurants place advertisements on their menus or in their bathrooms. These may seem like odd places to advertise, but they can be quite effective. Some professional organizers find this kind of marketing to be too expensive, but there's no harm in inquiring. An advertisement placed in a restaurant should not go into too much detail. It should include the name of the business, the contact information, and a brief description of the services offered. One cannot expect that diners are going to commit themselves to a close analysis of an advertisement they find on a menu or placemat.

Using newsletters
Many professional organizers place advertisements in the newsletters of local clubs and organizations. For instance, women's clubs and service organizations typically sell advertising space in their weekly or monthly bulletins. Placing these advertisements is rarely expensive, and it is a good way to reach a targeted audience. Also, many of these clubs and groups hold regular meetings with featured speakers. While inquiring about ad space, a professional organizer might offer to deliver a presentation. In some cases, the club will give an organizer complementary ad space in exchange for a brief speech. An organizer who can gain access to such a club or group will have a powerful tool for word-of-mouth business in the future.

Newspapers and magazines
One of the most traditional ways for professional organizers to market themselves is in newspapers and magazines. In a way, it is fitting for a professional organizer to advertise in the types of publications that tend to accumulate in a disorganized person's home. A professional organizer should only advertise in publications that are widely read by people in his or her target demographic. For instance, a professional organizer would not be wise to advertise

his or her services in a national current events magazine. Instead, organizers are advised to place ads in local or regional magazines and newspapers. Magazine advertising space tends to be slightly more expensive, but the ad will most likely get more attention over time. The advertisement should be designed with the publication's readership in mind. When marketing in a local magazine, for instance, the organizer should emphasize his or her connection with the community.

Advertising in the phone book

Advertising in the phone book can be expensive, but many professional organizers feel it is worth the cost. In order to place an advertisement in the Yellow Pages, a professional organizer needs to have a business phone line, which in itself is a significant cost. The rates for ad space in phone books tend to be large because these directories are only issued once a year. It is not terribly expensive simply to have one's name listed in the phone book, but placing a display ad can cost significantly more. Some phone books are now hosted online, where it is less expensive to advertise. For most professional organizers, it is better to wait before placing an advertisement in the phonebook. In some cases, though, obtaining a business line comes with the privilege of a brief listing.

Religious bulletins

One out-of-the-way place where many professional organizers find success in marketing themselves is religious bulletins. Many churches, synagogues, mosques, and other places of worship sell limited ad space in their weekly newsletters to local businesses. Placing an ad in a religious bulletin allows organizers to target a specific audience and present themselves as members of the community. Sometimes, several different religious institutions obtain their bulletins from the same printer, who also handles the advertising sales. In cases like these, a professional organizer can contact the printer and gain access to several different communities. Advertising in religious bulletins is often more expensive than advertising in newspapers or club newsletters, but it carries an appearance of class that will be appealing to many potential clients.

Resource directories

Many communities have resource directories where local professionals can advertise their services. For instance, there might be a resource directory for alternative medical practitioners or home improvement specialists. If there is such a directory in the area, a professional organizer would be well advised to advertise there. The organizer can be assured that anyone who looks at this advertisement is at least somewhat interested in learning more about organizational services. Resource directories can be especially useful for specialists. For instance, professional organizers who deal primarily with corporate clients could advertise in a directory for business services. In general, the rates for placing these advertisements are relatively low.

Television or radio

Television and radio advertisements reach a huge audience, but their costs can be huge as well. One way to slightly defray the cost of advertising on television is to place commercials exclusively on cable channels, as advertising on local network channels tends to be much more expensive. As for radio, a professional organizer may be able to get a better rate by advertising on an AM station rather than FM. Regardless of the station, any advertisement that is going to be placed on TV or the radio needs to be polished and professional. Most professional organizers do not have the skills to create an effective broadcast ad all by themselves. There are some ways to reduce the cost of producing an ad, however. One is to solicit the services of aspiring filmmakers or recording engineers. If there is a local university, the organizer might check with the film or marketing departments to see whether there are any students who would like to make a little money and gain some experience. Generally, television and radio ads are only a smart purchase for well-established organizers.

Web directories

There are several web directories for professional organization and related services. A web directory is a site that lists all of the service providers in a particular community. It is very important for a starting professional organizer to get listed on one of these sites, not only because it attracts clients, but because it gives the organizer credibility. Typically, there is some small cost associated with getting a placement on a web directory. After making the payment, the organizer fills out a brief form with all the information an interested party might seek. One of the great things about web directories is that they do not require an organizer to design an advertisement; all of the ads are arranged according to the same template. Most of these directories do not offer any preferential treatment to professionals, and so a beginning professional organizer can expect to receive the same placement as an experienced one.

Website ads and banner

A professional organizer may find success advertising on websites related to home improvement or organizing. Sometimes, organizers can trade ad space with other local professionals who offer complementary services. For instance, an organizer might let an interior decorator advertise on his or her site in exchange for a banner ad on the decorator's site. As with all Internet marketing, one of the huge advantages of placing website ads is

that it is possible to identify just how many people browse the site. In other words, the professional organizer can learn exactly how many people are intrigued enough to obtain more information. An organizer can then create a few different advertisements and see which one works best. Also, the organizer can investigate both the amount of traffic at various websites and the general profile of visitors. This information can be extremely useful for targeting marketing efforts.

Amount of money a professional organizer can earn

Professional organizers can do quite well for themselves, but financial success is largely dependent on drive and intelligence. Professional organizers make more money when they have more experience and are working with business clients. In a typical pricing scheme, an individual organizer will make between $50 and $150 per hour when working with individual or family clients, and between $75 to $200 when working with a business. In some cases, a professional organizer can make $2000 for a day of working with a corporation. Much of this depends on the project and the experience/expertise of the organizer. Organizers are often tempted to lower their rates in order to attract more clients. While this may be a good strategy for an organizer who is just beginning and looking to attract clients, underselling the competition for an extended period of time will send the wrong message about the quality of service being offered. A professional organizer should always set prices at least high enough to cover basic expenses.

Calculating likely income

An aspiring professional organizer will no doubt want to calculate the amount of money he or she is likely to earn. This is especially true for those who are leaving behind successful careers in other fields. To begin with, the new professional organizer should estimate the number of hours he or she will be able to work every week. Forty hours constitutes full-time employment, but personal circumstances may prevent an organizer from working this much. On the other hand, professionals without children or other responsibilities may be able to devote more time to their new job, particularly in the grueling start-up period. Unfortunately, however, professional organizers do not get paid for every hour they work, but only for those hours which they can bill to clients. For most professional organizers, only about half of the hours worked will be billable. So, if a professional organizer works 40 hours a week for 45 weeks out of the year (accounting for illness, holidays, and vacation), he or she will only have about 900 billable hours in a year. By taking this figure and multiplying it by various pay rates, the aspiring professional organizer can get a sense of his or her likely income.

Creating a professional organization business logo and design scheme

People who have strong organizational skills often have a good aesthetic sense as well, so selecting images to represent the business may be a fun task. The company logo and design scheme will be one of the first aspects of the business encountered by new clients, so it is important for it to be clean, clear, and engaging. Some professional organizers decide to hire a graphic designer to help with their logo, while others use computer drawing programs or even pen and paper to design their own. However the logo is developed, it should express the values of the company. That is, it should be simple and elegant. The last thing a professional organizer wants is a confusing, overly ornate logo that confuses potential clients and reminds them of the clutter in their

own home or office. Along with the logo, the personal organizer should select a font to use for his or her letterheads and business stationery. Again, this font should be distinctive but not too flashy.

Necessity of maintaining a post office box

Many professional organizers feel that it is unprofessional to list a home address on business correspondence. Some people are also concerned about the idea of giving their home address to strangers. For these organizers, setting up a post office box may be a good idea. The United States Postal Service offers very inexpensive mail service, and a number of private companies offer similar services. The post office is very reliable, but it may have slightly shorter hours and, for some people, a PO address suggests an untrustworthy business. Private mail service providers, however, give professionals a street address that is indistinguishable from any other brick-and-mortar business. Establishing an off-site address is relatively inexpensive, in any case, so it is often a good option for the beginning professional organizer.

Designing brochures

Every professional organizer will need to construct some basic brochures indicating the services he or she offers. Brochures can have several pages, so there's a tendency to fill every available space with information about the wonderful job the organizer will do. However, very few people will take the time to read every word in a brochure, particularly if they are not yet sure that they want to enlist the services of a professional organizer. Instead of filling the brochure with text, the professional organizer should focus on providing basic information and a set of attractive, informative images. It should also include all of the necessary contact information and office hours. The brochure should refer clients to the business website where they will be able to find more detailed information. Some professional organizers wait to create their brochures until their business is well established, at which point they expect to have a better idea of their services and availability.

Creating a website

Like all modern small business owners, professional organizers ignore the Internet at their own peril. It is becoming increasingly mandatory for professional organizers to establish a web presence. For those who are not experts in technical matters, however, this can be a daunting task. Rather than spend the time learning to design a website, a professional organizer may want to consider investing the money in a professional design. There are some simple, user-friendly website design programs, but the resulting product may be indistinguishable from other small business websites. An attractive website may pay for itself over time. Websites also require constant maintenance that a professional organizer may not have the time or inclination to perform. For most professional organizers, hiring a web designer is the best option.

An almost unlimited amount of information can be posted on a website, which can be a blessing or a curse for the professional organizer. There is a temptation to include everything related to the business, but this could be overwhelming to a first-time visitor. It is best for a website to have a clean, easy-to-navigate front page that allows visitors to explore the areas of their interest without wading through a great deal of irrelevant marketing material. A website should have plenty of pictures; many professional organizer websites have extensive before-and-after galleries. The website should also include a brief summary of the organizer's philosophy and the basic rates for different types of work and clients. It should include all of the essential contact information and hours of operation. It should probably include a brief personal description of the organizer so that potential clients will know who they are dealing with. One good thing about websites is that they can be adjusted over time, so the professional organizer is not committed to any bad decisions he or she makes initially.

Benefits of training and education programs

Even those professional organizers who were born to do the job may need some formal training or education before commencing business operations. There are a number of benefits to obtaining some basic training. For one thing, a general training program can indicate the many specializations within the field of professional organizing. Some new professionals may enter this line of work with a definite idea of what they want to do without fully understanding the options that are available. By learning more about possible services, a new professional organizer can learn to attract a broader range of clients. Another benefit of training and education programs is the opportunity to meet other professionals. These connections can be invaluable, especially at the beginning of a career.

Value of apprenticeships

One of the best ways for a beginning professional organizer to learn about the profession is to serve an apprenticeship under a more experienced professional. Working for a little while as an unpaid helper can be extremely remunerative over time because it will give the aspiring professional the knowledge needed to avoid all sorts of common mistakes and hassles. There are a few different ways to find a helpful older professional. One is to simply contact local professionals who practice in interesting areas. Another is to contact a professional association; these groups often arrange apprenticeships with a set of experienced and receptive pros. Serving as an apprentice is a great way to receive constructive criticism about one's own work and to learn about new areas of business. An apprentice also may gain access to future clients. Of course, it is important to always be respectful of the boss's business while serving as an apprentice.

Value of mentors and coaches

A beginning professional organizer can obtain a great deal of value from working with a mentor or coach. It does not necessarily need to be a professional operating in the same city or state; it could be a professional who has a similar specialty. Being mentored or coached is slightly different than serving as an apprentice. A mentor does not oversee the specific details of business operations, but rather provides general guidance on operating a professional organizing business. A mentor is a person that the beginning professional organizer can turn to in times of stress or confusion. Some professional organizers set up Internet-based communications with a mentor or coach; they e-mail pictures at the beginning of a project and ask the mentor for some general tips. This is a great way for a new professional to gain reassurance that he or she is doing a good job. Sometimes, getting confirmation from an older professional helps a beginning professional organizer trust his or her instincts.

Value of industry workshops

There are an increasing number of professional conferences, meetings, and workshops in the field of professional organization. Many community colleges offer brief courses in some of the areas that a professional organizer might service. All of the main professional associations have annual meetings at which there will be speeches and seminars for member professionals. In addition, many of these professional associations have local chapters which offer regular workshops and training sessions for professional organizers in the area. It is a good idea for a starting professional organizer to attend as many of these industry workshops as he or she can. Not only is this a great way to learn about the profession, but it is also a fantastic opportunity to meet other people in the field. There is no reason to be overly competitive with other professional organizers; in most places, if professional organizing services are adequately publicized, there will be plenty of work for everybody. A professional organizer remains interested in his or her work and keeps his or her skills fresh by regularly attending industry workshops.

Value of on-the-job training

There are all sorts of ways for a beginning professional organizer to learn his or her craft, but probably the best is simple on-the-job training. There are a number of informative books and DVDs related to professional organization. Many of these will be available from the local public library. Even those professional organizers who want to specialize in one area should be conversant in the other areas of the field. Now that there are many television programs devoted to organizing and household improvement, a professional organizer can expect that his or her clients will be at least superficially knowledgeable about the work. The professional organizer needs to be more informed than his or her clients. When a new system of organization becomes popular, a professional organizer needs to learn about it as soon as possible, because he or she can expect to be asked about it by clients sooner rather than later.

Value of certification

Professional organizers do not need to become certified, but many choose to do so anyway. There are several advantages of certification. For one thing, certified professional organizers can demonstrate to their clients that they have attained a high level of skill and knowledge in their field. If a client is not familiar with the organizer's previous work, he or she may be comforted by the organizer's credentials. In similar fashion, the professional organizer may gain a great deal of self-confidence from studying for and passing the examination. The National Association of Professional Organizers (NAPO) is the main credentialing body in the industry. Those who pass the NAPO examination become Certified Professional Organizers. A Certified Professional Organizer can be assured that he or she has the requisite knowledge base to be successful.

Impact of celebrity organizers

There are currently a number of popular home and office organization and improvement shows on television, which creates opportunities and challenges for the professional organizer. One positive consequence of these television shows is that the services offered by professional organizers are far better known than they were in the past, and so professionals have to do less public education and outreach. However, celebrity organizers give the public a somewhat warped view of the discipline. For one thing, on most of the reality television shows about professional organization, all of the work is done by the celebrity organizer and his or her crew without any input from the client. This model will not be very successful in the real world. Also,

television shows about organization tend to conclude after the project has been finished, so the viewer never gets a sense of whether the organizer's work actually translated into positive effects for the client. Celebrity organizers tend to use either the trendiest systems or the systems promoted by their sponsors, which can lead some clients and organizers to make poor decisions.

Offering gift certificates

Offering gift certificates may sound like a good way to bring in business, but a professional organizer should be wary of the type of clients they are likely to attract this way. A person who is given a certificate for professional organizing may not actually be interested in or emotionally ready for the process, which can make the work difficult for the organizer. One possible solution for professional organizers is to collaborate with a network of other home improvement and wellness professionals on gift certificates. In this model, a person can obtain a single gift certificate that allows the recipient to choose a professional from the network. This makes it much more likely that the clients who arrive by way of gift certificate will be committed to the process of organization. Professional organizers can even use these gift certificates in marketing promotions as a way of raising visibility and demonstrating membership in a professional community.

Content of a professional organizing advertisement

A professional organizer's advertisement should convey the essence of the services provided: it should be clean, simple, and efficient. The ad should be easily readable, so it is best to place either white letters on a black background or vice versa. A basic advertisement should include only those graphics that reinforce the mission of the business. The logo of a professional organizer should be elegant and attractive. It is also important for an advertisement to include some basic information about the business, like its name, phone number, website, and owner. The ad should include a brief description of the services offered, as well as any special prices or package deals available. A professional organizer's advertising should be uncluttered and free from excessive verbiage. When editing an ad, the organizer should weigh the value of each word, and only keep the minimum required to convey the point both clearly and persuasively.

Advertising expenses

When they think of advertising expenses, many professional organizers focus on buying ad space and forget about the cost of designing the ad itself. There are some ways to defray this cost. For organizers who do not want to design their own ads, it is often possible to obtain a discount by working with a certain publication's preferred graphic designer or marketing specialist. For instance, many magazines have creative people who assist businesses in creating effective advertisements. Of course, these people will be primarily concerned with creating an advertisement that can run in their particular publication. However, professional organizers can involve themselves in the process enough to create an ad that can be used both there and elsewhere. A professional organizer could also minimize the cost of ad design by working with students from a local college. Many colleges have marketing and graphic design programs full of students who would love to gain some practical experience.

Writing articles

In many ways, professional organizers are educators: they don't just solve problems for clients, they teach clients how to solve problems for themselves. One way that a professional organizer can combine educating the public with self-promotion is by writing articles for newsletters, newspapers, or magazines. Home improvement and organization publications are always looking for fresh voices. An experienced organizer is likely to amass a huge number of tips and strategies that would be useful to the reading public. Additionally, when the organizer's name is on the byline, the article is likely to attract new clients. Being published gives the organizer credibility in the profession, which can be self-perpetuating. For instance, organizers who are published writers are often contacted by other writers looking for quotes and background information for their work. The organizer's name will then appear in other articles, generating even more positive publicity. Organizers who are interested in writing articles should take notes of possible subject matter as they go through their professional life. Then, when it is time to write, the organizer simply needs to rework his or her notes into an interesting article.

Protocol for having an article published

Many professional organizers earn a little extra money and a lot of positive publicity by writing articles for magazines and newspapers. There are many publications that would be interested in the perspective of a professional organizer. Organizers may send their articles to a wide range of publications; once one of those publications accepts, however, the organizer must withdraw the article from consideration at the others. Payment for an organizing article is typically small, but the resulting exposure is almost priceless. Indeed, some organizers decline the writing fee in exchange for a more detailed byline. If the organizer can get the publication to include his or her contact information at the bottom of the article, the business generated will be exponentially greater.

Ways to elicit positive press

For a professional organizer, it is good publicity to write articles and even better publicity to be the subject of someone else's articles. However, eliciting favorable mentions in newspapers and magazines is much easier said than done. One way to put oneself in the public eye is to serve as an official on a local professional board. Another is to volunteer for a local service organization. There are all sorts of community events and institutions that could use the help of a professional organizer. By providing assistance *pro bono*, a professional organizer may generate lucrative business in the future. A more direct way of generating positive press is to collaborate with style or feature reporters on articles. A professional organizer could generate some story ideas and then contact the relevant reporters at the local newspaper. Some of these reporters will be starved for ideas and ready to listen to anyone with a fresh take on home improvement and decorating subjects.

Press releases and positive publicity

A professional organizer can use press releases to attract attention for his or her business. Many local newspapers and magazines include listings of current events in the community. By organizing and publicizing such an event, the professional promotes his or her business. Of course, press releases cannot be overdone: they should only be issued when the organizer has a genuine event to promote. Examples of press-release-worthy events are the opening of a business, the conducting of a workshop, or the delivery of a speech. In order for a press release to earn a mention, it must be demonstrably relevant to the publication's readership. In other words, a press release cannot be entirely self-serving; it must offer something of value to the potential client or audience member. A professional organizer should get in the habit of creating a press release any time he or she plans something that could be of interest in the community.

Contents of the typical press release

At the top of a typical press release are two important dates: the release date and the kill date. The release date is the time at which the press release is issued. A press release should not be issued too long in advance of the event in question or else it risks being ignored by the editor. The kill date is the time at which the information in the press release is no longer relevant. So, if a press release is issued for a speech delivered on January 15, the kill date would be January 16. Underneath the kill date, the press release should indicate its intended recipient, usually the community or current events editor of a magazine or newspaper. Below this will be the professional organizer's contact information (name, address, phone number, e-mail address, and Internet address). Then, the main part of the press release is a catchy description of the upcoming event. It is important for the press release to be crafted with the publication's readership in mind. Before sending a press release to a particular magazine or newspaper, the professional organizer should have a good idea of who is likely to read it.

Self promotion

Using panel cards
For professional organizers who do not have the time or inclination to create a brochure, a panel card can be a good alternative. A panel card is just a double-sided piece of thick paper on which the organizer lists his or her main services

- 16 -

and contact information. These cards may be displayed at restaurants, coffee shops, and other local businesses. Because they are simpler, they are much less expensive than brochures. Also, the printing options for panel cards are diverse, so it is possible to get a high-quality card for a low cost. As with brochures, it is important that a panel card be simple and appealing to the eye. It is an ideal place to display before-and-after pictures. A panel card should never try to be a comprehensive description of the organizer's services. Instead, it should intrigue interested parties and direct them to the organizer's website for more information.

Using business cards
Every professional organizer needs to have a set of business cards to give clients, potential clients, and any other contacts. Moreover, a professional organizer should always have some of these cards on his or her person because it is impossible to know when a useful networking opportunity will arise. Printing technology has made it possible to get text and graphics on both sides of an attractive card, so the organizer can give a list of services, basic contact information, and even a description of special offers. The business card is one area where the professional organizer should not try to conserve money. This card will be his or her representative in the world more than any other document or digital image, so it is essential that it be professional and attractive.

Using coupon packs
Some professional organizers promote themselves by placing vouchers in coupon packs. Coupon packs are the large envelopes of coupons sent through the mail. These packs are usually considered junk mail, but they can still generate a surprising amount of new business. Many professional organizers obtain a large portion of their new clientele through

direct mail campaigns and coupon packs. Of course, it is impossible to narrowly target an audience when creating coupon packs. However, the relatively low cost of advertising this way makes it less necessary to isolate particular recipients. Surprisingly, advertising in coupon packs can be effective even for professionals whose services are quite expensive. To advertise in coupon packs, professional organizers should look online for companies that put together these mailings.

Using direct mail
Direct mail is any advertising sent directly through the post to the thousands of addresses on a specialized mailing list. Each piece of direct mail costs very little money, but an entire direct mail campaign can be quite expensive. One of the most expensive aspects of this type of advertising is the purchase of the mailing list. Then, the organizer needs to design a glossy single-panel card for mailing. Finally, the organizer must pay the postage charge on every piece of mail. A professional organizer should only use direct-mail service when announcing a conference, workshop, or speech, or when opening a new business. A direct-mail ad that simply advertises professional organizing services is unlikely to generate any response. A professional organizer who is determined to use direct mail should consider postcards as a cheaper option. Also, it is important to obtain a mailing list that is appropriate for advertising professional organization services.

Using newspaper inserts
Many professional organizers advertise themselves by creating flyers that are placed inside newspapers. Newspaper subscriptions are down across the country, but older and more affluent people are still likely to receive the local paper, and these people are also one of the target demographics for professional organizers. It is easy to make a simple 8.5-

by-11-inch flyer on the computer. For about 10 cents per newspaper, the publisher will allow the organizer to insert these flyers. As with other forms of one-shot advertising, newspaper flyers are best used to promote a particular deal, to announce the provision of new services, or to herald the opening of a new business. Many professional organizers create newspaper inserts related to seasonal tasks, like spring cleaning or holiday preparation. Newspaper inserts can also be a great way to announce an upcoming workshop or lecture. In a newspaper insert, the professional organizer should remember that the people who will see it are not necessarily interested in obtaining the services of a professional organizer. Therefore, the flyer should have a minimum amount of technical detail, but should direct potential clients to a website for more information.

Posting flyers

One of the least expensive but potentially most successful forms of marketing is the creation and posting of simple flyers. Coffee shops, supermarkets, and schools are just some of the places that have bulletin boards where local businesses can advertise their services. The most successful professional organizers tailor each flyer to the type of person who is likely to see it. For instance, a school bulletin board would be a great place to advertise a back-to-school promotion. A local gift store would be a good place to advertise holiday preparation services. In many places, there is no charge for posting a flyer on the bulletin board, though it is common practice for the business to take down all of the flyers at the end of each month. Even when there is some cost attached, it is usually very small.

Branded items

Many small businesses promote themselves by putting their logo and contact information on small items like pens, notepads, and magnets. For a professional organizer, however, there is something contradictory about marketing through the very objects potential clients are likely to have in excess already. If a professional organizer feels compelled to place his or her business name on a product, probably the best option is a magnet. At the very least, these magnets can be used to affix paperwork to the refrigerator or file cabinet, somewhat reducing paper clutter. In general, though, handing out cheap souvenirs sends the wrong message. It is better just to stockpile attractive business cards.

Writing newsletters

Professional organizers who like to write can create all sorts of marketing opportunities for themselves. Many clients and potential clients will love to receive a regular update on new organization products, seasonal tips, and mentions of upcoming deals. It can be difficult to assemble a sufficient mailing list at first, but once an organizer becomes established, he or she should know enough interested parties to justify writing a newsletter. In the past, newsletter costs were prohibitive, but the presence of many inexpensive online publishing services has diminished this obstacle. Of course, many professional organizers don't see the point in creating a newsletter when it is possible to keep a blog basically for free. A blog can serve much the same function as a newsletter without creating any additional paper clutter.

There are all sorts of great ideas for a professional organization newsletter. One feature that readers love is profiles of happy customers. The organizer can write a brief narrative of his or her work with a particularly interesting customer and then display some before-and-after pictures. Another common feature is basic information about new organizing products. Some organizers devote different areas of the newsletter to specialties within the discipline, like paper management or kitchen organization. The newsletter could feature recommendations of books and websites related to organization. It is not necessary for organizers to create all of the content for a newsletter by themselves. For instance, an organizer could join with a colleague within the industry or from a related profession to create a newsletter with multiple perspectives and a wealth of interesting content.

Postcards

If a professional organizer is going to use a direct mail marketing campaign, it is advised that he or she send postcards. For one thing, the postage for a postcard is much cheaper. Also, when postcards are sent, envelopes are not necessary. A postcard campaign should be narrowly targeted. Most professional organizers only send postcards to their current or past customers. For instance, a professional organizer might send postcards to former clients every spring to remind them of a special offer on spring cleaning. It might also be a good idea to send cards around the holiday season to let former clients know that a professional organizer can help them get through such a busy time. Postcards can serve many of the same purposes as a business card: organizers can hand them out at networking events or after workshops. To be effective, a postcard needs to include some attractive imagery, like a dramatic set of before-and-after pictures.

Affixing a sign to car

It is trendy these days for small business owners to purchase a magnetic sign that can be affixed to the door of their car. This is an inexpensive way to attract attention, but it places a responsibility on the driver to keep the car clean and clutter-free. A professional organizer who advertises on his or her car can expect to have people peering in the windows. It is only natural that serious potential customers will be interested to see whether the interior of the organizer's car demonstrates the skills of a professional. For some organizers, this is a great incentive to keep the work car clean at all times. For others, though, it creates an annoying burden. Professional organizers who decide to purchase one of these signs should be sure that it contains all of the relevant contact information as well as a brief indication of services offered.

Importance of networking

To be a successful member of a small business community, a professional organizer needs to network often and well. Most cities and towns have networking events for independent professionals almost every week. These are opportunities for small business owners to socialize and spread the word about their businesses. Networking is especially important for professional organizers because many people in the community may not even be aware that such services exist. In order to make the most of a networking event, a professional organizer needs to bring a large number of business cards and other promotional materials. Attendees will be meeting a large number of people, so they need to have something to take home to remind them of the new professional organizer they met. After a few of these events, most professional organizers find that they are very comfortable discussing their business. Indeed, many organizers report that the confidence they obtain through networking translates into their interactions with clients.

Generating business through trade shows

Many professional associations put on trade shows, which are large-scale fairs or exhibitions where small business owners can set up booths to promote their services. For a fee, a professional organizer can rent a booth at a tradeshow. This has been demonstrated to be an excellent way to generate business. Of course, in order to be successful at a trade show, an organizer will need to have plenty of promotional materials. A booth needs to have some colorful pictures to draw people in and some detailed handouts to provide them with information. The professional organizer should also have some general information about the people who will be attending the trade show. The professional organizer should know how long the show will be open each day and, if necessary, should obtain some assistance running the booth. One common strategy of professional organizers at trade shows is to create a scene of clutter and disarray, and then show passersby some simple techniques for clearing it away quickly.

Using membership in business groups for promotion

Many professional organizers join groups of local small business people as a way of networking and generating business. Most cities and towns have a variety of small business associations that meet every week, every two weeks, or every month. The members of these groups commiserate about the joys and challenges of running a small business, and help each other with referrals. One great advantage of joining a small business group is learning to discuss one's business in a way that is comprehensible and entertaining to other people. A professional organizer may want to avoid joining too many groups, however, as this might dilute his or her enthusiasm. It is best to join just a few groups that are composed of professionals from related but not identical fields. For instance, a

professional organizer might want to join a group that includes interior decorators, event planners, and life coaches.

Enlisting the services of a public relations professional

To a beginning professional organizer, it might sound crazy to hire a public relations specialist. However, many professionals are surprised to learn that enlisting the services of a PR expert is not that expensive. Public relations professionals tend to have a broad amount of experience promoting different types of businesses. Also, there are PR agents who specialize in working with certain types of businesses. A professional organizer who is interested in hiring somebody to work on public relations should shop around. Most PR people will be happy to give samples of their work and describe how they would approach the professional organizer as a client. For most professional organizers, hiring a PR expert is something to think about once the business is well established. Nevertheless, it is a good idea to keep an eye on how these pros operate and determine the utility of their services for a growing business

Generating business through referrals

For most professional organizers, the largest share of their business is generated through referrals. The best way to earn referrals, of course, is to do good work. Professional organizers find that the amount of business they receive through referrals increases exponentially: the more business they generate through referrals, the more referrals they get in the future. One of the greatest things about referrals is that they don't cost any money in most cases. A satisfied client or other professional will usually be satisfied with a thank-you after they recommend the professional organizer's service to an interested party. It is important for the professional organizer to thank those who provide them with referrals, though. This is not only the right thing to do, but it encourages future referrals. Some organizers send gift baskets or other small tokens of appreciation to people who refer clients.

Creating a marketing plan

In order to be successful in promoting his or her business, a professional organizer needs to compose a marketing plan. Indeed, many people think that the marketing plan is even more important than the business plan in the early stages of operations. The marketing plan does not need to be a complicated document: it can be as short as a single page. Also, marketing plans are always subject to adjustment. The first step in the creation of a marketing plan is a list of possible promotional strategies. The organizer should research possible ways to publicize his or her business and then decide on those that appeal to him or her. After this, the organizer needs to obtain some specific information about these modes of promotion. The organizer should determine how much time and money each of these methods will require. The organizer will want to prioritize his or her approaches because time will be limited during the early stages of the business. Also, the organizer may not have enough money to afford some of the more enticing forms of advertisement.

Contents of the marketing plan

A professional organizer's marketing plan does not need to be comprehensible to anyone other than himself, but it is important that it include some basic information. For instance, the marketing plan should indicate the number of hours per week that the organizer wants to work. It should also name a date by which the organizer plans to have accumulated a set amount of work. A marketing plan should also indicate, if appropriate, the number of speaking engagements and workshops the organizer wants to have scheduled by a certain date. Having established these targets, the marketing plan should then detail the methods of attaining them. The organizer's top three marketing strategies should be listed on the worksheet. Below the name of each strategy should be a brief description of the clients it will target. Then, the organizer should indicate how much time and money each marketing strategy will require. The final component of each marketing strategy entry is a short list of tasks to be completed in the near future in order to get started.

Contents of the typical marketing evaluation document

Smart professional organizers are constantly evaluating the success of their marketing strategies. The best way to do this is by creating a marketing evaluation worksheet. At the top of this document will be a brief description of the marketing strategy, as for instance television spots, newsletters, blog, and so on. Then, the organizer will indicate how much this marketing strategy has cost in both time and money. The marketing evaluation worksheet should then indicate the number of clients and hours that were obtained as a direct result of this marketing strategy. Of course, this information can be difficult to obtain, so it is very important to ask new clients how they heard about the business. The professional organizer should also indicate any other business opportunities that were created by this marketing strategy. On most marketing evaluation documents there is a space for the organizer to decide whether he or she believes this marketing strategy has been successful. There should also be a place where the organizer can indicate possible adjustments to the strategy, should it be used again.

Required office supplies

Professional organizers will need certain office supplies to conduct normal business operations. To begin with, a professional organizer will need basic utilities, like Internet, telephone, and voicemail services. In terms of technology, professional organizers need computers and may need special software as well. For an office, a professional organizer needs a desk and chair, and needs filing cabinets for holding paperwork and client information. A professional organizer will need a printer and plenty of paper for paperwork. For routine office duties, he or she will also need basic office supplies, like staplers, paper clips, and post-it notes. A professional organizer will send out a lot of correspondence, so he or she will need handsome stationary and some decent pens. Finally, a professional organizer will need some kind of bag or case in which to carry his or her materials. Professional organizers need to be able to take equipment along with them to the work site.

Basic expenses

A professional organizer will need to own a car, and this car will need gas and insurance. A professional organizer will also need to pay for advertising and marketing, particularly at the beginning of his or her career before he or she has acquired a solid base of clients. When starting out, a professional organizer must pay to register his or her business, and must pay banking fees associated with transactions. Some professional organizers will opt to become members of a professional organization, in which case they will need to pay dues and other fees. Some professional organizers obtain certifications and licensures in the field,

and the exams can be expensive. On occasion, a professional organizer may need to obtain counsel, and legal fees can be quite expensive as well. Those professional organizers who choose to handle their own finances will probably need to buy accounting software. Finally, professional organizers must continue to improve their skills, so they will sometimes need to pay for training, further education, and consulting.

Basic operating costs

Professional organizers do not have extreme amounts of overhead compared to other small business owners, but they do have some basic operating costs. For instance, a professional organizer can expect to spend about $25 a month on accounting services. Professional organizers often need to maintain a post office box, which can cost about $10 a month. For technological purposes, professional organizers need web hosting ($40 per month), phone service ($35 per month), cell phone service ($50 per month), and electricity ($60 per month). They will likely have to pay banking fees and insurance premiums, which can cost up to $100 a month. Professional organizers may also need to pay for supplies on a monthly basis, and this can cost about $50. For most professional organizers, however, the biggest monthly cost is advertising. Professional organizers typically spend about $200 every month on ads. In all, a professional organizer can expect to spend approximately $500 per month on operating costs.

Demands of a professional organizer

Emotional demands
Being a professional organizer sounds soothing, but it can be a very emotionally demanding job as well. Leaving aside the work itself, being a professional organizer entails all of the responsibilities and

stresses that afflict any small-business owner. Most professional organizers do not make a great deal of money at first, and it can be difficult to establish a client base. Professional organizers must often work long hours, especially when they first open the business. They are subject to the whims of their clients, many of whom are naturally disorganized and difficult to control. A professional organizer will need to have large reserves of patience in order to handle the inevitable but unforeseen problems of the profession. Even the daily work of a professional organizer can be stressful. A professional organizer may be juggling several clients at the same time, and may need to rethink his or her own organizational skills before arriving at a suitable system for handling business.

Physical demands

A professional organizer is likely to expend significant physical energy in just the normal course of business. Professional organizers are always on the move, especially those who deal with cluttered and constricted physical spaces. At the beginning of a project, a professional organizer is likely to be working in a space that is ill suited to freedom of movement. Many professional organizers are required to lift heavy objects in the normal course of their business. Regardless of what type of work a professional organizer is doing, he or she will be taxed mentally by interactions with clients and the challenges of difficult projects. A professional organizer needs to have healthy habits in order to manage the stresses of the job. It is a good idea to have a regular exercise program and some stress management strategies in place before beginning work as a professional organizer.

How clients and professional organizers find one another

For a beginning professional organizer, one of the most daunting tasks can be attracting new clients. Every professional organizer needs to engage in continuous marketing and advertising efforts in order to generate leads and establish name recognition. Still, many pros are surprised at how many of their clients contact them because of their own desire, not because they are lured in by ads. People seem to know when they need the help of a professional organizer and will seek one out when they are ready. Much of the point of advertising and marketing is to ensure that clients will know how to find a professional organizer when the time is right. Also, professional organizers can improve their chances of finding clients by educating the public about exactly what they do. Many people who would love to enlist the services of a professional organizer may not even know that such a job exists. As more people learn about professional organizers, the demand for their skills will increase.

Importance of creating a business plan

Before starting out, a professional organizer should document his or her ideas and intentions in a business plan. The business plan does not have to be an elaborate document; a few pages ought to be enough. It should be comprehensive and detailed, though it should be adjusted frequently once it comes into contact with reality. The business plan should begin with a brief description of the business to be created. This should be the clearest summary of what the business aspires to accomplish. It should also include some reasons why the business is appropriate for the person starting it. To be successful, a professional organizer needs to be honest about why he or she is getting into the field in the first place. The business plan should also indicate some specific objectives for the business. This could be phrased in terms of number of clients, hours of work per week, or earnings. The business plan should include some ideas for how the business will grow in the future, and may indicate the ultimate desired size of the business.

Establishing a separate work space

Many professional organizers work from their homes, which can be a blessing and a curse. Waking up in the morning and walking directly from the bed into the office is convenient, but it can also make work responsibilities and home life difficult to separate. This is especially true for professional organizers who are also parents. It is important to create a physical distinction between work and home, even if it is just a door or a screen. Some professional organizers are lucky enough to have a separate space, like a garage or guest house, adjacent to their home. A professional organizer must have some sort of structure that will keep them from being interrupted by spouses or children. Also, it is a good idea to have a separate phone line for the work environment so that business cannot be interrupted by personal matters.

Setting up phone service

Phone service varies by region, so the first step for any beginning professional organizer when setting up utilities should be to check with the provider. Some companies offer special rates for small business owners. It is typical, however, for a business account to be slightly more expensive than a residential account. For a little over $100 a month, a business receives a listing in the phone book and referrals from the phone company's information service (that is, people who call information looking for the business will be given the number). If the extra cost of a business is line is prohibitive,

however, a fledgling professional organizer can always just add another residential line. When outgoing calls are made, the caller identification system of the person being called will register the name of the professional organizer rather than the name of his or her business.

Professional organizers are required to spend a great deal of time on the phone: discussing ideas with clients, setting up deals with manufacturers, and handling the day-to-day work of running a small business are all routine tasks. It is important that the phone not only be a different line than the home phone, but that it be physically separate from the home phone, as well. A professional organizer's business phone should be kept in his or her office, and the office should not have a personal line. The professional organizer should have a separate voicemail service for business calls so that the outgoing message can refer to the name of the business. For professional organizers who work from home, it is essential that the business line is inaccessible from the living space; one does not want a spouse or child to pick up the line by accident and interrupt a business call. It is also a good idea for the professional organizer to restrict the business phone line to the office so that he or she is not tempted to make or answer business calls before or after work hours.

Choosing between an answering machine or a voicemail service

It may be tempting to use an answering machine that is already in the house, but it is far better for a beginning professional organizer to pay a little extra money to receive the voicemail service offered by the phone company. In most cases, the supplemental charge for this service is very small. Also, a voicemail service offers many advantages over an answering machine. For one thing, a voicemail service is accessible from any phone line, whether at home, the office, or elsewhere. Also, the outgoing messages on voicemail services tend to be clearer, which creates a better presentation for clients. Voicemail services are able to respond to calls that come in while the line is in use, so the client will not be stuck with an annoying busy signal. Although it is a good idea for professional organizers to obtain a basic voicemail service, it is usually bad to also receive call waiting. Being interrupted in the middle of a call can be distracting and disrespectful to the client. If a voicemail service is in place, incoming callers can always leave a message.

Outgoing voicemail message

When a professional organizer is unable to take a call in person, the outgoing message represents his or her business to the world. It is essential, then, for this message to be clear, informative, and professional. A fledgling organizer should not just record the first message that comes to mind. The message should be composed on paper, read aloud to others, and edited before it is used professionally. Some professional organizers elect to change their outgoing messages frequently to reflect office hours or upcoming vacations. Indeed, some professional organizers change their messages every time they leave the office. When a client calls, he or she wants to talk with a real person as soon as possible. Recording an informative and current outgoing message reassures the client that the organizer will be back in touch with them soon. The message should always include some direct reassurance, like the phrase, "Your call is very important to me." Also, rather than simply saying that no one is available, it is more useful to indicate when someone will be able to return the call.

Setting up a toll-free number

Some professional organizers decide that establishing a toll-free number gives their business a classy or impressive appearance. However, this is usually an unnecessary step for a beginning business. For one thing, beginning professional organizers can expect to be doing most of their business with people who are in their area code, so there is no benefit to the client in having a toll-free number to call. In rare cases, a new professional organizer will be offering their services across a broader geographical region, and it may be a good idea to set up a toll-free number. Even then, though, this is a step that does not need to be taken until the business is well established. For some local clients, a toll-free number may even be discouraging, as they may think that it indicates a lack of connection with the community.

Cell phone

A professional organizer absolutely must have a cell phone. Much of the work of a professional organizer is done away from the office, so there must be some way for him or her to stay in touch with clients and business connections. Some professional organizers, however, elect not to give their cell phone number to clients. One reason for this decision is that some clients can be very aggressive about demanding attention, and can prevent the organizer from operating efficiently. Another reason, though, is that cell phone coverage and voicemail services can be erratic, and so a client who leaves a message on a cell phone might have to wait hours before receiving a return call. A professional organizer certainly wants to avoid alienating a client in this way. Even if clients don't have the number, a cell phone will have constant utility for the professional organizer. For instance, it can be used to find directions or alert an awaiting client about a possible delay. A cell phone also makes it possible for the professional organizer to put any downtime to use, like returning phone calls or placing orders for equipment.

Points of cell phone etiquette

A cell phone can be an invaluable tool for a professional organizer, but only if certain rules of etiquette are observed. To begin with, a professional organizer should always turn his or her cell phone off when meeting with a client. The client deserves to have the undivided attention of the professional organizer during any time for which he or she will be billed. Besides, it is simply bad manners to check a cell phone or answer a phone call while in conversation with another person. Some cell phones have special settings that allow the user to establish a unique ring tone for emergency calls. Another crucial point of cell phone etiquette for professional organizers is to avoid driving and talking on the phone at the same time. Although this is becoming increasingly illegal anyway, it is also poor manners. A client should always feel like he or she is receiving the full attention of the professional organizer, which the professional organizer cannot provide if he or she is driving.

Fax machines

In the past, much of the paperwork associated with professional organizing was transmitted by fax machines. Now, as the Internet becomes omnipresent, there is very little use for these outmoded devices. Many professional organizers continue to keep fax machines in their offices, but they probably get very little use. In the rare event that a fax does need to be sent or received, it is possible to do this at a package store for a very low price. This eliminates the need to pay for the machine, its supplies, and repair. In almost every case, scanning and e-mailing a document will be the preferred mode of transfer for clients, dealers, and other professionals.

Computers

Many starting professional organizers are surprised to learn that a computer is not an absolutely essential item for the home office. There are some very useful programs related to organization, most notably spreadsheet programs, but virtually all the functions that a computer can perform can also be accomplished manually. Most professional organizers like to keep hard copies of their files on hand, so maintaining a computer record as well is not always necessary. Of course, computers are everywhere now, so it is likely that a professional organizer will already own one and be able to put it into service. Professional organizing does not require an extremely fast processor or a massive hard drive. A computer should be quick and reliable, however. Computers can be very useful for keeping in touch with clients, though this can also be accomplished with a smartphone. The vast majority of professional organizers will use a computer system, but all should be aware that this is not absolutely necessary.

Important computer features

When a professional organizer shops for a computer, he or she should be aware of the unique needs associated with the profession. For instance, many organization computer programs are graphically based, so it can be useful to have a large monitor with good resolution. Professional organizers are often on the move, so a laptop or netbook is usually a better option than a desktop model. A computer will need to have a basic, easy-to-understand word processing program, as well as database and spreadsheet programs. Many professional organizers do their own accounting, and there are several quality programs for this purpose. Professional organizers who are not computer savvy should obtain a long warranty and a comprehensive technical support plan.

Computer problems can strike at any time, and they can be debilitating for people who are untrained technically. It is essential to be able to call upon assistance around the clock and on weekends.

Computer system backup

Many professional organizers keep all of their files and records on computers, so suddenly losing the contents of a hard drive can be devastating. It is absolutely essential to back up all computers frequently. No matter how smoothly a computer is running, or how much money it cost, it will inevitably have problems. There are a number of different ways to back up the files on a computer. One is to purchase an external hard drive and regularly upload the contents of the computer hard drive to it. Another is to subscribe to one of the increasingly popular online services that host customer data. These services store almost unlimited amounts of information on multiple servers, making them very reliable. This method is probably better than storing data on a secondary hard drive at home, because it protects the professional organizer from losing data in a fire, flood, or other catastrophic event.

Maintaining a client database

Professional organizers are constantly meeting new potential clients and dealing with current clients, so they need to have a system for maintaining client information. This is especially true because many projects will have strong similarities, and so it can be easy for the professional organizer to confuse them. In addition, professional organizers will need a system to handle all the contacts they make at networking events and conferences. Probably the best way to maintain all of this information is to establish a computer database. There are a number of good programs available for a minimal cost. The professional organizer should select the one that

seems the easiest to use and that comes with the most comprehensive technical support plan. The program should allow the organizer to find client records by point of initial contact, first or last name, company, or address. Sometimes, it can be difficult for the organizer to recall a potential client's name or situation. The database system must be able to help with this problem.

Individual client information

A professional organizer needs to keep all of the basic and useful information about a client on hand in a database. The database entry for an individual client should include his or her name, home phone number, cell phone number, address, and e-mail address. It should also include the names of the client's spouse and children, if he or she has such relations. Database entry should also include some more detailed information, like the reason for the initial contact with the client and any important events in the relationship. For those professional organizers who maintain a mailing list, the database should include an indication of whether the client would like to receive mailings. Most computerized database programs will be able to locate client records when any of this information is entered into a search window.

Corporate client information

A professional organizer needs to keep all of the essential and useful information related to corporate clients in a reliable and searchable database. The database entry for a corporate client should include the name of the company and the name and title of the person with whom the professional organizer primarily does business. It should also include the basic contact information for the company: its physical address, phone number, website address, e-mail address, and (if relevant) fax number. It should also include a brief description of the initial meeting with the corporate contact. There should be a description of the contact's original problems and desires. There should also be a record of any ongoing conversation between the professional organizer and anyone at the company. Finally, if the professional organizer maintains a mailing list, there should be an indication of whether the business would like to receive mailings in the future.

Collecting fees

At first, a professional organizer may only be able to accept payment in the form of cash or checks. Once the business is more established, it can afford to accept credit card payments. The protocol for collecting payment varies. When a client purchases a package deal, it is customary for payment to be made before services are provided. When a client pays by the hour, most professional organizers prefer to be paid at the end of each work session. Some organizers feel comfortable issuing bills to their clients and then collecting a lump sum in the future, but this may create problems when the business is just beginning and has limited cash flow. Also, many professional organizers feel uncomfortable having to remind a delinquent client of outstanding payments. The best way to avoid these problems is to notify clients at the beginning of the project that payment must either be made in advance or at the conclusion of each session.

Establishing boundaries between work and personal life

In this age of constant accessibility, it can be difficult for any professional to establish boundaries between work and home. Many professional organizers work at home, however, which makes the task even harder. If there is not adequate separation between work and home life, both areas may suffer. Family members can feel neglected if the professional organizer brings his or her work home,

and clients can become frustrated with an organizer who seems distracted by personal problems. The best way to create the necessary boundary is to establish regular work routines and adhere to them. Family members should know when the professional organizer is at work, and when he or she is available for them. Only in emergencies should this routine be broken. Whenever exceptions are made, the professional organizer should take care to remind other people of the agreed-upon routines. It can be useful to hang a sign on the home office door to indicate whether it is appropriate to enter.

Importance of discipline

Professional organizers are typically self-employed, which can be a dream so long as there is sufficient discipline. Otherwise, whole days can be frittered away on insignificant and trivial tasks. For a starting professional organizer, it is especially important to establish strict work habits. The professional organizer should determine the number of hours he or she needs to work every week, and then should adhere to that schedule no matter what. It can be useful to publicize the planned schedule so that family members and friends can help the organizer maintain it. Sharing work goals with other people also creates an incentive to succeed and not disappoint others. Of course, establishing overly ambitious work goals can be a recipe for failure. It may be necessary to work for a week or two before deciding what is a fair and realistic target. For instance, many professional organizers find that they are exhausted at the end of the day, so this could be a good time to complete unfinished paperwork and other light tasks.

Legal and Ethical Considerations

Discussing confidentiality with clients

There is an expectation of confidentiality when dealing with professionals like doctors, lawyers, and therapists. A professional organizer should extend the same courtesy, though the client may not be aware of it. For this reason, the organizer should be explicit about his or her policy on confidentiality. At some point during the initial meeting with the client, the organizer should state that any information about the client will remain anonymous and free of identifying detail. Organizers will often share stories about former clients, but they should never name them. In some cases, a client will indicate that he or she does not mind having identifying information passed on to others; even so, there is no reason for the organizer to disclose personal information unless necessary. On the other hand, some clients will be a little sheepish about having solicited the services of a professional organizer, and so the organizer should be prepared to keep his or her work confidential.

Showing respect to clients

It is very important for a professional organizer to be respectful of clients. For instance, a professional organizer should never make negative or sarcastic comments about the client's clutter or level of disorganization. The professional organizer should always treat the client's possessions with a great deal of respect. Clients may have special rules for visitors, like a prohibition on shoes or on food and drink in certain areas. It is important for the professional organizer to inquire about and respect these rules. Part of the work of a professional organizer is to take objects out of storage and sort them into piles. However, the organizer needs to ensure that this is done with the utmost respect for the objects. Objects should never be placed on the ground except with the permission of the client, and it is usually a good idea to lay down towels or blankets first.

It is important for a professional organizer to maintain a formal and polite tone when communicating with clients. A professional organizer should never use foul language or make off-color jokes. This is true even with clients who themselves speak coarsely; the organizer must always maintain the elevated tone of a professional. In similar fashion, a professional organizer needs to respect the personal boundaries between himself and the client. The professional organizer should neither volunteer excessive or irrelevant personal information nor pry into the client's affairs except in the context of the shared work. At times, it will be appropriate for a professional organizer to share some personal details, but this should only be in the service of providing the client with context for services. The professional organizer should never force the client to discuss issues that make the client uncomfortable.

Rules for communicating with clients

A professional organizer must always maintain a civil tone when communicating with clients. The professional organizer should never express himself in an overly judgmental way. In the early stages of a project, the professional organizer may encounter a great deal of disorganization and clutter. Under no circumstances should the organizer make cutting remarks or sarcastic jokes about the client's space. More generally, the professional organizer should always ask questions rather than make assumptions. Questions should be pitched at the comprehension level of the client and sensitive to the client's desires and concerns. A professional organizer who has a great deal of experience may project his or her knowledge base on the client, and therefore believe that the client automatically understands everything the organizer does. Of course, this is rarely the case, so the organizer needs to articulate even the most obvious points of assessment and planning.

Maintaining the client's privacy

A professional organizer must use extreme caution and courtesy with regards to the privacy of clients. By the nature of the job, a professional organizer will obtain a great deal of information, both personal and otherwise, about clients. However, this information should not be shared with other people except with the client's permission. It is a good habit for a professional organizer to omit a client's name when describing the project to other people. Including the name or other identifying information of the client adds nothing to the story. Other professional organizers and potential clients will be discouraged by someone who makes negative jokes or is excessively critical of clients. If a professional organizer finds it difficult to avoid speaking harshly about clients, he or she may want to consider a different line of work.

Process of selecting a name for a professional organizing business

The name of the business may be the most important early decision a professional organizer makes. When thinking of a name, the professional organizer should consider the image he or she wants to create for clients and potential clients. It is useful if the name lends itself to graphic representation, as on the logo. It should be easy to pronounce and understand because the professional organizer will be saying it over the phone frequently. It should be distinctive and give some indication of the services provided. It should be appropriate for the target audience; for instance, it should not use slang if the target market is not likely to understand it. It is a good idea to check whether the proposed name is available as a dot-com web address. Before settling on the name, a professional organizer should probably perform an Internet search on it to make sure that it is not already taken or that there is not some other negative association with it.

Necessity of selecting a unique name
Many professional organizers believe that they have discovered the perfect name for their business, only to discover later that it is already taken or that it has a negative association of which they were unaware. Before finalizing a name decision, the professional organizer should always discuss his or her choice with friends, family, and some other local professionals. The organizer should also run the proposed name through a few different Internet search engines, both to see if it is in use by other professional organizers or if it produces distasteful search results. Everyone knows that there is a great deal of seediness on the Internet, but a professional organizer does not want potential clients to be reminded of this fact every time they search for his or her business. Finally, the professional organizers should enter the proposed name as one word followed by a ".com." If another business' webpage appears, the professional organizer should probably find a different name.

Registering the new business

If the proposed name for a new professional organizing business does not produce any negative Internet search results, the professional organizer should begin the process of registering in his or her city, county, and state. The registration offices for all of these governments will have extensive lists of registered businesses, so any similarities with existing businesses will be identified immediately. In some states, it is only necessary to register a new business at the city level. This may be no more difficult than filling out a short form and paying a small fee. The professional organizer will also be required to indicate the name under which he or she is doing business. In almost every case, this will be the person given's name. In some rare circumstances, a person may want to do business under an assumed name, which is known in business as a DBA ("doing business as"). Professional organizers who are interested in providing services in other states or across the nation will need to either register in all the states in which they plan to do business or trademark their business name. Otherwise, these organizers will be subject to lawsuits from distant businesses with the same name.

Value of trademarking the name

Many professional organizers elect to trademark the name of their business even if they are not planning to offer services outside of their home state. This will prevent people from using the organizer's business name or anything similar to it. At present, it costs about $400 to trademark a name. It is typical to hire an attorney to assist with the process, which usually expands the cost to over $1000. However, acquiring a trademark for the business name can be an invaluable form of insurance over time. Having to change a business name because of legal action from another professional can result in thousands of dollars of paperwork, as all business correspondence and printed material will need to be altered. By trademarking, a

beginning professional organizer can avoid a crisis in the future.

Creation of a business entity

For tax and legal purposes, a business must be defined as having a certain structure. This decision must be made at the beginning of the business formation process, though it may be changed in the future. Bank accounts cannot be established until the business has defined itself. There are a few different options for professional organizers. The most common types of business are sole proprietorships, partnerships, and corporations. There are also specific types of partnership and corporation that may appeal to certain professional organizers. With regard to all of these business structures, the primary considerations for a professional organizer will be personal liability, taxation, and simplicity. A personal organizer wants to select the option that will least endanger his or her personal assets, will result in the most favorable tax treatment, and will be the easiest to initiate and maintain.

Sole proprietorship
Sole proprietorship is perhaps the most common legal structure for independent professional organizers. A sole proprietorship is extremely simple to establish, with very little paperwork required. A sole proprietorship is owned and operated by a single person. The owner of a sole proprietorship does not receive a salary from the business, but is free to extract funds for personal use whenever he or she likes. However, the owner of a sole proprietorship is liable for the debts of the business, so if the business were to default on loans, the personal assets of the proprietor could be seized. Running a sole proprietorship requires very little adjustment to taxes; the only addition is Schedule C of Form 1040, which aligns business income with personal income. Most professional

organizers begin as sole proprietors, in part because this is the simplest route and in part because they have amassed very few liabilities yet. It is important to note that the phrase "sole proprietorship" does not mean the business may not employ other people.

Partnership

A personal organizing business should only be operated as a partnership when more than one person is involved. In some ways, a partnership is similar to a sole proprietorship because the operators are the owners of the business, and they are legally and financially responsible for their liabilities. Indeed, partners are responsible for one another's actions, and can be prosecuted jointly. When a partnership is formed, it is important to solicit the input of an attorney. A partnership agreement should indicate how profits and losses will be distributed, how responsibility will be shared, and how the partners will deal with liabilities. It should also indicate the contingency plans in the event of prolonged illness, death, or disability. There should also be a plan in place in case one of the partners wants to leave the partnership in the future. Partnership agreements are usually subject to future revision.

For professional organizers who want to work together, a partnership can be an extremely beneficial business structure. Partners can share the basic costs of operating a small business, from office space and equipment to advertising and conference fees. Also, partners can help each other in times of excessive workload. Many professional organizing partnerships are composed of people with different skill sets who can assist one another on difficult projects while remaining focused in another area. Also, in a partnership, professionals can take vacations at different times so the business never has to shut down. Taxation does not become much more

difficult when one enters into a partnership; all that is required is filling out a Form 1065 for the company and a supplemental K1 for each partner's personal taxes. The respective tax burden of each partner will be established in the partnership agreement.

Corporation

Although very few personal organizers begin by incorporating, many successful professionals eventually do so later in their careers. A corporation is different from a sole proprietorship or a partnership in that it is defined by the government as an entity distinct from the owners. This means that the corporation itself can be sued and taxed, and that it is liable for debts separate from the operators. The owners of a corporation are its shareholders. One advantage of the corporation model is that it is easier to raise funds. Instead of having to get a loan from the bank or use his or her own personal savings, a professional organizer can simply sell more shares of stock in the business. Starting a corporation requires extensive assistance from accountants and attorneys. For this reason, it is not a very good option for the beginning professional organizer.

Limited liability company

Some beginning professional organizers decide to structure their business as a limited liability company, or LLC. A limited liability company is a slightly more organized version of a partnership. It requires the filing of an initial business agreement, as well as a series of forms and meetings with state authorities. As the name suggests, a limited liability company restricts the extent to which the personal assets of the owners can be targeted by creditors. Many people choose to file as a limited liability company because they want to avoid the liability of a partnership while retaining the preferential tax treatment. Nevertheless, limited liability companies do require more tax paperwork than partnerships or sole proprietorships. There is also a version of the limited liability company for single operators, known as the sole member LLC. This may be a good option for independent professional organizers.

Types of insurance required

During the formation of a professional organizing business, many people forget to purchase insurance. However, without proper insurance, a professional organizer can be held liable for all sorts of problems whether they are his or her own fault or not. Professional organizers make all kinds of decisions, and they can be held responsible when these decisions go wrong. The first and most important type of insurance, then, is basic liability insurance. This can be obtained often through professional organizing associations that offer discounts and specialized coverage. Professional organizers may also want to investigate the following types of insurance: fire, general property, life, health, disability, errors and omissions, workers' compensation, and auto. In some cases, car insurance rates increase when the vehicle is used for business as well as personal tasks. In lieu of disability insurance, a professional organizer might want to obtain business interruption insurance, which will help them maintain some income should they suffer a debilitating illness or injury. Most professional organizers will not elect to obtain all of these forms of insurance at first. It is a good idea to obtain basic coverage and then see how the business develops and what types of insurance are appropriate.

Business property insurance
Professional organizers who run their businesses from home may be required to purchase additional homeowner's or rental insurance. Similarly, professional organizers who work from an office may need to purchase business property insurance. This kind of coverage is particularly useful if the office or workspace is going to contain inventory of products or supplies. It is also a good idea to obtain this type of coverage when the office will contain extremely valuable business equipment. For instance, if a professional organizer has a top-quality computer system, a photocopier, and a flashy printer, he or she may want to be insured against the loss of this equipment due to property damage. It is a good idea to discuss the value of this insurance with a representative from a professional association or a trusted insurance provider.

Necessity of bonding

When a professional is bonded, it means that he or she is capable of repaying debts immediately. For instance, if an accident should occur at a client's home or office, a bonded professional organizer would be able to guarantee repayment. This guarantee is based on regular payments made to a bonding company, which would immediately compensate the property owner. The next step would be for the professional organizer to repay the bonding company. Bonding functions like insurance, except it ultimately leaves the organizer responsible for the entire amount of liability. The issue of bonding rarely arises except in work for corporate clients. For most professional organizers, it is unnecessary to get bonded unless specifically requested to do so by a client. In order to be bonded, the professional organizer will have to submit to a background check. Becoming bonded is not a bad thing, but it is not necessary to do so until asked.

Setting up business bank accounts

Before beginning operations, a professional organizer needs to establish business bank accounts. The first step is to shop around: professional organizers should find a bank with comprehensive online account access and excellent customer service. A professional organizer should also inquire about monthly account administration fees. These fees are often larger for business clients than they are for personal accounts. At some banks, however, individuals who already have personal accounts may open the account for a reduced rate. Also, some banks offer merchant accounts, which enable the professional organizer to be paid with credit cards. These accounts can be more expensive, but the convenience they offer to clients will result in more business in the future. Many clients will prefer not to pay with cash or check. It can take a few days to set up a business bank account, so it is good to take care of this task well in advance of opening the business.

Use of personal and business checks

Most banks offer several different business checking systems. For instance, banks may offer a large desktop check register with individual receipt tabs. These systems provide all of the necessary forms for checks, but they are not portable. Also, desktop check registers typically do not provide carbon copies of checks. Having an automatic duplicate can be useful for a professional organizer who is less than diligent about recording transactions. Of course, checks are used far less often in business transactions than they were in the past. It is much more common for clients to pay with a credit or debit card. Indeed, professional organizers should make sure that the business bank account they choose has a debit card associated with it. Debit cards are extremely convenient, though they do not allow the holder to spend more money than he or she has in the account. The professional organizer must be aware of his or her balance to avoid bouncing a debit card purchase.

Basic bookkeeping system

Bookkeeping is the process of recording every monetary transaction of a business. It is absolutely imperative that a professional organizer maintain accurate and current books, not only to make paying taxes as easy and painless as possible, but to provide insight into the inflow and outflow of money for the business. Bookkeeping can be a tedious process, but it has become less so with the introduction of easy-to-use computer programs. The professional organizer will need to make a note of every receipt, deposit slip, invoice, and statement. It is a good idea to get in the habit of storing all receipts and deposits in the same place. Many of these slips will be acquired outside of the office, so the professional organizer should routinely empty his or her wallet or purse upon returning home. Every purchase that is made while acting as a professional should be recorded. In some cases, the organizer will be reimbursed for purchases made on behalf of a client, but this is impossible unless the receipt is saved.

Basic bookkeeping is more a matter of diligence and good habits than skill. Nevertheless, many people prefer to avoid this task entirely. Professional organizers who recoil at the idea of keeping their books in any form may hire a part-time bookkeeper. For the rest, there are a few different options. Some professional organizers elect to keep their books the old-fashioned way, in journals and ledgers. There is something reassuring for some people about having all of this information in a hard copy. However, it is much faster and more efficient to use one of the inexpensive software programs now available. These software programs allow the user to take a look at his or her finances at any point. They also allow the user to isolate certain types of transaction so he or she can see the specific areas in which money is entering or leaving the business. Of course, keeping books on a computer makes the user subject to all of the normal risks. This is yet another reason to regularly backup the contents of the hard drive.

Employer identification number

Every business that is either incorporated or pays wages to one or more employees is required by the Internal Revenue Service to acquire an employer identification number (EIN), often referred to as a tax ID number. Sole proprietors do not need to acquire an employee identification number; they may use their Social Security number instead. Employee identification numbers may be obtained at the Internal Revenue Service website for free. These numbers are used to identify businesses. It usually takes about one month to receive an employee identification number from the IRS, though the process may be expedited by submitting the application by fax instead of mail. It is important to have an employee identification number before filing a business tax return. For this reason, any professional organizer who plans on incorporating or thinks he or she might need to hire employees during the course of the year should acquire an EIN.

Quarterly estimated income taxes

Professional organizers are typically self-employed, meaning that nobody is withholding taxes from their income as it comes in. Self-employed professionals are required to pay a portion of their income tax every quarter, mainly because the government does not trust everyone to set aside enough money to pay only once a year. Any professional who expects to owe more than $1000 in income taxes is required to make an estimated quarterly tax payment. The amount of the payment can be calculated using IRS publication 505 (*Tax Withholding and Estimated Tax*)

and Form 1040–ES. Organizers who have never spent much time with tax forms may find it worthwhile to consult with an accountant at this point. The quarterly estimated tax payment is due on the 15th of January, April, June, and September. Business owners who fail to make an estimated quarterly tax payment may be subject to penalties.

Self-employment and sales taxes

In addition to income taxes, a self-employed professional organizer will need to pay for Social Security and Medicare. The amount of tax may be calculated with IRS Form 1040, Schedule SE. Every professional who has an income higher than $400 is required to pay these self-employment taxes. At last check, these taxes amounted to 15.3 percent of income up to $94,200. The rates are subject to change, however, and it may be worthwhile to consult an accountant on this issue. Self-employment taxes are due on April 15. Professional organizers who sell products as part of their business are required to assess, report, and pay a sales tax. In order to do this, the professional organizer needs to obtain a state resale certificate. This process usually only takes a few days. Each state has a specific protocol for calculating and paying sales tax. Again, it may be worthwhile to consult a professional before delving too far into this issue.

Taxes that are required to be paid if employees are hired

A professional organizer who hires employees becomes liable for several different taxes. These taxes are for income, Medicare, Social Security, and unemployment, and are collectively known as withholding (FIT), FICA, and FUTA. The process of paying these taxes begins when the employee is hired. At that time, the employee will fill out a W-4 form and claim a certain number of exemptions, otherwise known as withholding allowances. The exemptions and the amount of tax levied are combined to determine the amount of money withheld from the employee's paycheck and sent to the government. At the end of the calendar year, the professional organizer will need to draft a W-2 form for each employee. A W-2 form provides a summary of the employee's income and withholdings over the calendar year. The IRS mandates that employees receive a copy of this form by January 31. Another copy must be sent to the Internal Revenue Service itself.

Claiming the business use the home as a tax deduction

Professional organizers who run their businesses from their homes are eligible for a number of different tax deductions. The ever-increasing number of professionals working from home has forced the IRS to become more flexible about these deductions. In other words, professionals who claim deductions based on the business use of their home are no more likely to be audited than those who rent their office space. Of course, this does not mean that professional organizers should misrepresent themselves on tax forms. It is important to keep accurate and comprehensive records in order to support the deductions claimed. In order to receive these deductions, the organizer's home office must be either a room or a part of the house that is regularly and solely used for business purposes. In other words, the home office must be an office only, and not the kitchen table. It is also required that the home office be the primary place of business for the professional. Finally, the home office must be the place where the professional does or would meet with clients in the normal course of business. It is not necessary to demonstrate that these meetings occur often, only that the home

office would be the natural place for them to occur.

There are several deductions associated with using part of one's home for business. For instance, any improvement made to the home office is eligible for tax deduction. If new carpet is put down in the home office, the entire cost may be deducted. However, the cost of putting a new roof on the entire house would not be deductible. Rather, the professional organizer would have to calculate the percentage of the roof that covers the home office; only this portion would be subject to deduction. There are a couple of different ways to calculate the percentage of the home used by the home office. One is to calculate the percentage of the house's total square footage covered by the office. Another is to calculate the percentage of the total rooms in the house that are used for the office. These percentages are used to determine the portion of utilities, real estate taxes, insurance premiums, depreciation, and mortgage interest associated with the home office. All of this information is reported on IRS Form 8829, *Expenses for Business Use of Your Home.*

Miscellaneous allowable deductions

In addition to deducting expenses related to the home office and car, a self-employed professional organizer may be able to deduct his or her advertising and promotional expenses. In some cases, a professional will be able to deduct the cost of office supplies and equipment. Professionals may be able to deduct the fees or annual dues associated with membership in a professional association. They may also be able to deduct the cost of any continuing education or training they participate in throughout the year. With the help of a savvy accountant, many professional organizers are able to deduct their telephone and Internet expenses. It is also possible to get a tax deduction for insurance premiums and the interest on money borrowed for the exclusive purpose of continuing business operations. Finally, a professional organizer may be able to deduct any fees he or she pays for professional advice or consultation.

Tax deductions related to vehicle expenses

Self-employed professional organizers can usually deduct at least some of the expenses related to the vehicle they use for business. There are two different ways to calculate this deduction; the professional organizer should perform both calculations and select the method that results in the larger deduction. The first method is to multiply the number of miles driven in the performance of business tasks by the current tax deduction rate. This rate changes every year, so it will be necessary to research it at the IRS website or to ask an accountant. The second method is to determine the amount of money spent on vehicle expenses and add it to depreciation, or the rough amount by which the value of the vehicle has decreased due to normal wear and tear. In order to calculate the amount of money spent on vehicle expenses, it is necessary to keep all records associated with gas purchases, repairs, parking fees, towing charges, and routine maintenance. It can be difficult at first to remember to keep all these records, but the amount of money saved at tax time makes it worthwhile.

Recording business use of a vehicle

In order to maintain accurate records related to the business use of a vehicle, and thereby to become eligible for a tax deduction, a professional organizer needs to develop some good habits. For one thing, the organizer needs to obtain a receipt for every purchase associated with the vehicle, whether for gas, repairs, tolls, or parking. It is a good idea to obtain a special gas credit card so that all fuel purchases will be recorded not only in receipts obtained at the pump but in a statement from the card company. An even more exacting process is keeping track of mileage. This is especially difficult when the same car is used for business and personal errands. One way to do it is to keep a notebook in the car, and write down the odometer reading at the beginning and end of each trip. Another is to use an online map service to find the precise mileage to each destination, and then record the distance traveled in a notebook in the home office. All of these methods require diligence and persistence, but they can save the professional organizer a great deal of money over time.

Filing a tax return

The difficulty and complexity of filing a tax return as a professional organizer depends in large part upon the selected business structure. Sole proprietorships and limited liability companies report earnings and deductions on the individual tax form (1040). The profit and loss of a sole proprietorship is indicated on supplemental Schedule C, while Schedule E is used for limited liability companies. In addition, limited liability companies must submit Form 1065, which is the business tax return. Business tax information is required for the completion of personal tax forms, so it is necessary to calculate business taxes before completing one's personal return. Tax preparation can be a very complicated process, particularly for a beginning professional, so it may be worthwhile to enlist the services of an accountant, at least for the first few years of operation. The cost of hiring an accountant to prepare business tax returns varies depending on the location and the size of the business. Typically, though, it runs from a few hundred to a few thousand dollars.

Internal Revenue Service publications that could be useful

Filling out business taxes for the first time can be a daunting task for the beginning professional organizer, so it is important to acquire as much guidance and supplemental information as possible. There are a number of publications from the Internal Revenue Service that can be invaluable for the fledgling professional. Publication 334, *Tax Guide for Small Business*, is a comprehensive look at filing business taxes. Publication 505, *Tax Withholding and Estimated Tax*, is a guide to making the quarterly payments required for self-employed professionals. Publication 533, *Self-Employment Tax*, provides a general summary of tax issues for independent professionals. Publication 534, *Depreciation*, indicates the amount that equipment and other property can be devalued annually. Publication 535, *Business Expenses*, indicates the purchases that may be eligible for tax deductions. Publication 583, *Starting a Business and Keeping Records*, is a general introduction for the beginning professional. Publication 917, *Business Use of Your Car*, describes the deductions that may be obtained for vehicle costs. Finally, publication 587, *Business Use of Your Home*, describes the set of deductions related to maintaining a home office.

Keeping client forms to a minimum

A professional organizer should avoid overburdening clients with paperwork. After all, many of these clients will have contacted the organizer in the first place because of a problem with paper clutter. If the client does not yet have a good system for organizing and managing paper, it is not likely that the bills and worksheets transmitted by the organizer

will be the exception. Whenever possible, the organizer should send paperwork and documentation over e-mail so that the client will be less likely to lose it. Some professional organizers don't give their clients any paperwork at all. Instead, they maintain all of the important documentation in a file folder that they bring with them to every client visit. During the visit, the client is given access to all of the paperwork. A professional organizer may want to adjust his or her form strategy to the individual client.

Client intake form

At the beginning of every organizer-client relationship, there should be a client intake form. On this form, the organizer records all of the most important information about the client, including contact information and the reason for their interest in organizing services. The client intake form is to be filled out by the organizer in most cases, although it can be a good idea to have the client review it and make additions or changes. Typically, the organizer will begin filling out this form while on the phone or meeting in person with the client. The organizer may take note of key words and specific information as the client talks so that he or she may go back and complete the form in more detail later. The professional organizer should be able to refer to the client intake form later and obtain a comprehensive view of the client's original problem.

Contents
A typical client intake form has the business letterhead at the top. Underneath the document title is a space for the client's name, address, and phone number. This is also a good place to indicate the date of initial contact between the client and organizer. Many organizers like to indicate how the client initially discovered the organizer. This can be useful for future marketing efforts.

Under this will be space for more detailed information about the initial conversation with the client. For instance, the organizer may want to take notes about the client's description of his or her problem. There should be a space indicating the immediate steps to be taken by the organizer, whether visiting for an assessment or scheduling a future meeting. Below, the organizer may want to record a brief description of the client and his or her family. The organizer should record any information that he or she believes could be useful in the future and which he or she might forget. Finally, the organizer may want to briefly outline a possible strategy for serving the client.

Working agreement form

After first meeting with the client, a professional organizer needs to devise a working agreement form. The working agreement form establishes the basic expectation for the client as well as the professional courtesies guaranteed by the organizer. Specifically, a working agreement form will indicate the policy for making and canceling appointments, the typical rate of pay, the policy for travel reimbursement, and the scope of service provision. Some professional organizers are more comfortable with a very elaborate working agreement form, while others provide one that is simple and more flexible. A professional organizer may decide to personalize the working agreement form by including his or her initial assessment notes. This can be useful if it indicates to the client the reasons for setting a particular rate or limiting service in some way.

Contents

The typical working agreement form issued by a professional organizer has the company letterhead and logo at the top. Below the title of the form is space for the client's basic information: name, address, phone number, e-mail address, and date of initial contact. Then, there will be a summary of the plan agreed upon by the organizer and client. This form will be filled out before the project commences, so it is important to note that the plan is provisional and subject to change. However, for the benefit of the client, the professional organizer should try to be as detailed as possible in this section. Next, the organizer will want to make a basic estimate of the schedule required to complete the project. The rate at which the client will pay should also be indicated. Finally, the back of a working agreement form usually details the business policies of the professional organizer. At a minimum, the form should discuss the policies for making, confirming, and canceling appointments, as well as the travel reimbursement policy.

Work record form

Of all the forms created by a professional organizer, the work record is probably the most labor-intensive. It is the record of all the hours spent and tasks accomplished during each meeting with the client. On long projects, the work record may stretch over many pages, so it is usually not a good idea to issue a copy to the client. However, the client should be aware that he or she has total access to the work record. Clients may want to review the work record to get a sense of where they are on the project path. To be useful, the work record must be comprehensive and detailed. It must include all of the dates and hours worked, as well as a full description of the progress made during each meeting. It must also include a record of payment. In rare cases, a client may dispute the amount or existence of a certain payment, so it is good to record this information and review it with the client at every meeting.

Contents

A typical work record form has the company's logo and letterhead at the top. Underneath the form's title will be a space for the client's essential contact information: name, address, phone number, and e-mail address. Underneath this will be a space for the rate at which the client is paying as well as the payments received thus far. Then, the main part of the sheet will contain a detailed account of the work sessions. Each session should be identified by its date, time, and number of hours worked. There should be a space for the organizer to briefly describe the work accomplished during that session. Some organizers keep a running countdown of the estimated number of hours left on the project along with each entry. On long projects, it is possible that the work record will run to several pages.

Giving clients homework in between work sessions

Some professional organizers like to keep their clients involved with the project between work sessions by assigning them "homework." This will be either a task to be completed or an issue to be meditated on before the next meeting. For instance, the organizer might ask the client to create a list of items that need to be purchased in order to complete the project. In another scenario, the organizer might ask the client to think about whether there are personal issues underlying bad organizational habits or clutter. Obviously, homework assignments will not be graded, and the organizer should not penalize the client if he or she cannot complete the assignment in between work sessions. However, if the client seems uninterested in the homework, the organizer might want to have a discussion with him or her about the necessity of commitment to the process. Homework assignments are an

especially good idea when there will be long gaps in between meetings.

Providing paper proposals

Professional organizers seldom need to put a work proposal in writing when dealing with private clients. Most of the information that would be covered in a work proposal is included in the initial assessment and work record forms. If the client agrees to a particular rate of pay, there is usually no need to formalize this agreement in a paper proposal. When dealing with corporate clients, however, a formal proposal is often mandatory. This is because the corporate contact may not be the person whose approval is required to begin work. The boss may need an "executive summary" that he or she can scan before giving permission. A professional organizer who wants to work with business clients should be prepared to create work proposals for those clients. The typical work proposal includes an invoice and a summary of the services to be provided.

Contents

Work proposals are rarely required except when dealing with corporate clients. A typical work proposal includes an invoice and a summary of the services to be provided. The invoice begins with the businesses logo and letterhead. Underneath those is space for the date, the name of the client, and the client address. Then, there should be a brief explanation of the fee structure. The invoice should indicate when payment is due and whether it may be subdivided into smaller portions. Many professional organizers choose to include a brief note expressing appreciation for the client's interest. The remainder of the work proposal is a summary of the planned services. It should define the organizational problem as well as the intended solution. It should include an indication of how long and how frequently the organizer will need to work to accomplish the goal. It should also include any relevant business policies, like the protocols for making, confirming, or canceling appointments.

Contents of a work proposal for a speaking engagement or training program

Experienced professional organizers may be asked to speak about their services and philosophy in front of a paying audience. It is typical for the organizer to issue a brief proposal in advance of such a presentation. This proposal typically includes all of the basic information about the organizer, such as his or her contact information and fee structure. The proposal should also include the title and theme of his or her presentation. Any special supplies or equipment the professional organizer needs in order to deliver the presentation should be listed on the work proposal. Even if the professional organizer will provide the equipment himself, it is important to identify it so that the host can arrange the necessary utilities. Finally, a work proposal for a speaking engagement or training program should include a brief summary of the organizer's business policies.

Sending invoices

Professional organizers are not obliged to send invoices to their clients, but many choose to so that accounts receivable will be on record. Some professional organizers only send invoices to their corporate clients. Typically, an invoice lists the services to be provided and the agreed-upon rate of pay. It is issued after an acceptance of the work proposal by the client. In essence, an invoice formalizes the relationship between the organizer and client. It is especially appropriate when dealing with clients who have many business transactions going on at the same time, and therefore may have difficulty keeping them all straight. Most financial accounting and word processing programs include invoice templates. It is recommended that organizers date the invoice from the initial day of service, as this will leave the invoice record in the most logical order when it is reviewed at the end of the year.

Issuing receipts

Many professional organizers are used to getting a receipt every time they make a purchase, and so they naturally assume that they will need to issue receipts to their clients upon being paid. However, there is no real obligation to generate a receipt for each payment. In fact, most professional organizers find that clients are not very interested in receiving another piece of paper. The services of a professional organizer are not tax deductible, so there is very little reason for a client to save receipts except possibly to balance his or her bank account. It may be a good idea to purchase a receipt book in case a client requests a receipt, but professional organizers will rarely be called upon to do so. A simple receipt book can be attained at any store that sells stationery or office supplies.

Products that a professional organizer can make independently

Some professional organizers offer educational products in addition to their hands-on work with clients. Professional organizers are educators, and they can promote their work through many of the media traditionally used for teaching. For instance, many professional organizers put together booklets or workbooks compiling all of the basic information related to common organization projects. Other organizers assemble handy lists of useful products that clients can refer to after the project is complete. A beginning professional organizer will probably not have enough knowledge to create an effective teaching tool, but by paying close attention to recurring themes, he or she can begin to identify the essential organizing wisdom that each client will need to have. Many veteran organizers have unique workbooks for clients with kitchen problems, paperwork issues, and difficulty preparing for special events.

Market recordings of speeches and workshops

Many professional organizers earn part of their income by delivering speeches and leading workshops for local audiences. This income can be dramatically increased by recording these performances and offering them for sale to clients. Once an organizer has refined a presentation, it can be professionally recorded for a surprisingly low cost. For instance, it typically costs about $1000 to have a professional video team record and edit a presentation of three or four hours. There will be some additional expense for producing a sellable recording, but the increase in prestige and income for the organizer can be significant. Once the presentation has been recorded, the organizer can sell copies of it every time he or she delivers another speech or leads another workshop. Audience members who are impressed by a presentation are often interested in purchasing a copy that they can watch again.

Generating income by selling products on the website

Many professional organizers create an additional income stream by selling products on their websites. Retailers of organization products often have affiliate programs that allow their products to be sold on another business' website. When a professional organizer registers as an affiliate for a retailer, the organizer receives a sales commission every time someone purchases one of the retailer's products through the organizer's website. The organizer can learn more about these affiliate programs by visiting the retailer's site and searching for an affiliate information page. Each company has a unique agreement with its affiliates, but these follow a general pattern. In some cases, the organizer posts pictures of the products and creates links to the retailer's website, while in other programs the organizer can handle more elements of the transaction.

Preliminary Assessment

Assessment phase of an organization project

The first step of any organization project is assessment. During this phase, the professional organizer collects information about the client and his or her organization dilemmas. The assessment phase begins at the initial contact between the client and the professional organizer. It is important for the professional organizer to record as much information from this initial conversation as possible. It is during the first conversation that the client will likely be most expressive and idiosyncratic in his or her description of the problem. That is, this will be the point at which the client has not yet acquired the vocabulary of professional organization, so he or she will speak most personally. As a professional organizer gains experience, he or she will learn to interpret the vague and sometimes confused language new clients use in an initial conversation. A professional organizer should also ask many questions at this initial interview to gain a complete understanding of the client's mental and emotional state.

Preparing for an initial assessment
Even experienced professional organizers are often nervous before an initial assessment meeting. The best way to allay these concerns is to be fully prepared. A professional organizer should leave plenty of time to get to the client's home or office. The organizer does not want to be undone by getting lost or stuck in traffic. The organizer also needs to have the following materials: intake form, client folder, map to the jobsite, business cards, working agreement form, digital camera, and table of rates. This, of course, is all in addition to the normal materials the organizer should have in his or her work bag. It is very important that the organizer be on time for the appointment. Many organizers even like to arrive a little early so that they can gather their thoughts and relax before the beginning of the assessment.

Beginning an initial assessment
Although the professional organizer may be nervous before an initial assessment, it is likely that the client will be even more so. One of the professional responsibilities of the organizer is to mitigate the client's concerns as soon and as much as possible. A smile and a friendly handshake are crucial. Before the assessment begins, the organizer should conduct a brief interview. If the client offers a drink, the organizer should feel free to accept; sometimes these gestures of hospitality establish a more intimate connection between professional and client. However, the organizer should make it clear that he or she has brought water and a snack, and that the client is not responsible for taking care of his or her personal needs. Once the organizer and client have settled into a comfortable place for conversation, the organizer should briefly review their initial conversation. If the client wants to make any adjustments to his or her original complaint, this is the time to do so. This pre-assessment conversation is a way of reaffirming the shared goals for the project.

First interaction with the client
A beginning professional organizer may be excited about starting operations but unsure about how to handle his or her first client conversation. When a client calls, the first thing the organizer should do is learn why. That is, the organizer should ask the client what aspects of hiring a professional organizer are attractive. The organizer should then make a general inquiry about the client's organization problems. Based on the

client's response, the organizer should probe for more specific detail. An organizer should never agree to perform services just for the sake of having business, but instead should ensure that his or her talents are aligned with the client's needs. After getting a general idea of the client's situation, the organizer should outline the basic course of the project. Most clients are not aware that a professional organizer needs to make an initial assessment before creating a plan. If the client still seems interested after services have been described, the organizer should describe the structure for payment. If the client agrees, the organizer should arrange an initial meeting. Finally, the organizer should offer to answer any of the client's questions.

Touring the client's home or office
After having a brief conversation with the client to reinforce shared goals, the professional organizer will want to tour the home or office. During the tour, the professional organizer should ask questions. Specifically, he or she should ask the client to describe the strengths and weaknesses of the target spaces. It is a good idea for the organizer to take notes during this tour because he or she will be absorbing a great deal of information and might not be able to recall all of it later. The organizer should ask the client how the particular spaces are used and what the essential items for these uses are. The organizer should get the client to discuss his or her organization problems and also his or her desired solution.

Avoiding a narrow focus
A client's organization problems may seem overwhelming, and there can be a tendency to become overwhelmed by the details of certain key problems. It is important for an organizer, however, to limit the focus on specifics during the initial assessment. This is a time for obtaining a detached, distant view of the

client's problems, not for excessive analysis. Spending too much time on individual aspects of the client's organization problems can result in a failure to see more general trends or patterns of behavior. To use a medical analogy, the initial assessment is the time for diagnosing the client's illness, not for treating his or her individual symptoms. By addressing the issues that underlie all of the client's organization problems, the organizer can solve a range of smaller problems simultaneously. Moreover, an initial assessment should not last more than an hour and a half or so. A longer visit may exhaust the client.

Agenda and schedule
It is important for a professional organizer to limit the duration of an initial assessment meeting, in part to avoid exhausting the client. In general, the entire meeting should take no more than an hour and a half. After arriving, the organizer and client should have a brief introductory conversation of about 10 minutes. The main part of the meeting will be a tour of the problem space. This should take somewhere between 45 minutes and an hour. Afterwards, the organizer will need about 10 minutes to complete the assessment form, and the last 15 minutes will be spent on some concluding conversation and arrangements for subsequent meetings. As a professional gains experience, he or she will become better at staying on schedule during the initial assessment. No matter how large or complex the problem, the organizer should strive to keep the initial assessment brief.

Records that should be made
After going on an initial tour of the client's home or office, the professional organizer will need to sit down and draft an assessment form. Like the tour itself, the assessment form should be general in its scope. It should include a rough estimate of how long it will take to complete the

project, along with a summary of rates. It should include any general observations the organizer made during the tour as well as a set of tasks the client may execute before the next meeting. It is often a good idea to give the client a few basic questions to ponder before the project begins. Sometimes, a client will contact the organizer without having a clear idea why. At all times, the organizer should press the client to articulate his or her goals for their work together.

Being courteous

Even though a full plan has not yet been created, a professional organizer should view the initial assessment as the beginning of the project. When touring the client's home or office, the organizer should take whatever steps he or she believes are necessary to get a comprehensive view of the problem. Of course, the organizer should remain courteous at all times. For instance, it may be necessary for the organizer to open some of the client's drawers in order to gauge the amount of clutter. The organizer should always ask before doing so. It will be impossible for the organizer to estimate the length of the project without some such investigation. The organizer should always be sensitive to the possibility that a client may be reluctant to have his or her possessions examined or handled by a person he or she just met. In most cases, though, the client will understand the need for the organizer's intrusion and will quickly become accustomed to sharing.

General suggestions to make to the client

Some professional organizers believe that it is inappropriate to make suggestions during an initial assessment. They feel that the assessment should be entirely devoted to discovering the nature of the client's problem. Really, though, there is nothing wrong with providing some tips while touring the client's home or office. Professional organizers should not be worried about revealing trade secrets once they are dealing with the client. On the contrary, giving the client a sample of practical wisdom will encourage the client to commit to the project more fully. If the client gets the sense that the organizer is knowledgeable and perceptive, he or she will be much easier to deal with during the course of the project. The intention of an organizer should always be to teach the client how to become an efficient and self-sufficient person.

Discussing the project details

Once the organizer and client have finished touring the targeted space, the organizer should complete the assessment form and discuss the project details with the client. The organizer should answer any questions the client may have about schedule and rates. The organizer should always emphasize that schedules are estimated and subject to adjustment once the project begins. The organizer should stress that it is important to set aside large blocks of time for the project so that a great deal of work can be done with a minimum of setup and cleaning. If the client can only meet for one or two hours at a time, it will significantly increase the overall duration of the project. The organizer and client should agree on a schedule for the next two or three meetings. It is best to have the next meeting as soon as possible in order to build on the momentum created during the initial assessment. If possible, the organizer should arrange to meet with the client at the same time every week to create a sense of routine and commitment.

How to elicit the client's concerns

In most cases, it is not difficult for a professional organizer to get a new client to discuss his or her organizational problems. However, it takes empathy and experience to have the client describe these problems with the insight required to create permanent solutions. At first, a professional organizer should simply let the client speak frankly about his or her organizational problems. When the client has finished his or her summary of the situation, though, the professional organizer should ask some specific questions. For instance, the organizer might ask the client why he or she dislikes a particular space, if there are any aspects of the space and how it is used that are especially abhorrent to the client, or whether there are certain items that the client has difficulty finding or cannot decide where to put. These questions are good at isolating the specific complaints of the client. It is also important for the professional organizer to follow these questions with more detailed inquiries. The organizer wants to know not only what the client thinks, but why.

Helping the client define priorities
During the initial assessment, the professional organizer needs to attain a sense of what the client values. There are all sorts of ways to solve an organizational project, but not all of them will be compatible with the client's personality and priorities. For instance, some clients will be focused on the appearance of a physical space, while others may view improvement as a strictly practical matter. Part of the assessment phase should be a complete inquiry into the client's favorite objects, activities, and aesthetics. The client should be able to name the most important items in the physical space or else the professional organizer will not know to redesign the room around these objects. It is amazing how often clients give special placement to objects they either dislike or rarely use. If a client can be encouraged to reduce the most important things and activities for the given physical space, he or she will be able to collaborate on a solution that accentuates these favorites.

Handling requests to speak with former clients

Obtaining the services of a professional organizer can be a significant expense, and many clients will want to perform due diligence before signing on. This may lead them to request an interview with one or more of the organizer's former clients. Unless it is absolutely impossible for some reason, the organizer should acquiesce to such a request. An organizer should have several former clients who are willing to testify to the quality of his or her service. If the organizer is just starting out, he or she may need to provide some complimentary services for family and friends in order to generate these positive references. In most cases, if a former client was satisfied with the organizer's work, he or she will be happy to give a recommendation. The professional organizer will want to build this list of references continuously so that some former clients do not become tired of giving positive reviews.

Discussing past work history

Potential clients are often curious about a professional organizer's work history. A professional organizer should be able to summarize some of his or her past projects upon inquiry. Of course, this line of questioning can be problematic for a professional organizer who is just starting his or her career. This is yet another reason why it is a good idea to gain some experience completing projects with family and friends. Anyone for whom the professional organizer has provided services in exchange for payment can be considered a client. Even so, a professional organizer with limited experience may be unable to satisfy the potential client's curiosity. If the potential client seems unsure that the organizer has enough experience, the organizer should simply assert his or her confidence and allow the client to decide whether to go forward.

Discussing educations and training

Potential clients will often be curious about the professional organizer's training and education. This can be a difficult subject for professional organizers who have not completed a formal certification program. Although the skills of a professional organizer are largely self-taught and even intuitive, it is important that a professional be able to cite specific influences on his or her development. This may be as simple as a set of books or an apprenticeship that the organizer served. The organizer may want to discuss some of the industry leaders whom he or she aspires to emulate. Even when a professional's experience is limited, he or she can at least convey strong passion for the subject. If the organizer can speak with clarity, detail, and enthusiasm, it is likely that the client will overlook the shortcomings of his or her formal training.

Reassuring an uncertain or reluctant potential client

Many potential clients are unsure about soliciting the services of a professional organizer. A client may feel that his or her situation is unique and that even an experienced organizer will be overwhelmed by it. A client may also feel that his or her situation is hopeless or that it is rooted in problems beyond the scope of a professional organizer. While the organizer should not try to persuade someone to pay for services they don't need, it is a good idea to reassure the client about the almost universal utility of professional organizational services. Clients who suspect that their organization problems are rooted in deeper mental and emotional issues may be pleased to learn that organizing the

external space can make it possible to organize internally. Also, a professional organizer should be able to reassure the client that, even though his or her mess is unique, it is still susceptible to the same organization strategies as any other.

Value of assessing the client's strengths

Too often, professional organizers consider and deal with clients solely as people who have organizational problems. However, every client has strengths and talents, and tapping into these can be extremely important in creating an organizational solution. Clients will naturally be fixated on their problems or else they wouldn't have contacted a professional organizer in the first place. Still, it is a good idea for the organizer to inquire about the things the client believes he or she already does well. If the client is concerned about the way a particular space is being used, the organizer might ask the client to describe the things about the space that the client likes. Those aspects of the space could then be accentuated in the plan. When evaluating a client's strengths, the professional organizer should be as specific as possible. For instance, he or she could ask the client to describe activities for which the physical space is already well suited. Even when the client does not directly answer the question, his or her response will give the professional organizer information about his or her values. The plan eventually created by the professional organizer should be aligned with the client's personality.

Importance of avoiding making assumptions

The number one mistake made by new professional organizers is rushing to accomplishment. That is, new professional organizers are still uncertain of their skills and so they have a tendency to leap to conclusions and implement solutions before they have been given adequate thought. It is very important to spend a great deal of time assessing and questioning the client so as to avoid making faulty assumptions. A good professional organizer has to be a good listener; often, there are personal or psychological issues underlying what appear to be purely physical problems. For instance, a client may complain about excessive clutter that the new professional organizer believes can be resolved simply by throwing things away. A more extensive interview with the client could reveal, however, that the underlying cause of the client's clutter is an inability to confront some personal problem. If the professional organizer does not listen to the client, he or she risks devising a solution to a problem that doesn't exist.

Clutter

Clutter is essentially any item that does not have a place where it can be put away when it is not being used. Clutter is all of the items that accumulate on surfaces, whether tables, counters, or chairs. Clutter is essentially any item in the home or office that is not used or appreciated. Any object that does not add value to the owner's life in some way is considered clutter. Items that have to do with half-finished tasks are considered clutter, and indeed this type of clutter can be particularly troublesome because it makes the owner anxious about not having finished the job. Any item that needs to be repaired or processed is considered clutter until it is taken care of. Any item that the owner plans to discard but has not yet gotten around to discarding is considered clutter. Whenever a collection of items with different uses is jumbled together, clutter is created. Some items will always be clutter, while others can be a valuable

part of the home or office with a little work and consideration.

Reasons people accumulate clutter
People accumulate clutter for all sorts of reasons. Some people think that they will one day get around to using a certain object, though that day rarely (if ever) comes. Many people think that they will eventually get around to using a product, or that it is a bad idea to throw something away while it is still good. However, a disorganized person needs to consider whether the item may still be good, but not good for him or her. It is also not a good idea to keep something around just because it might someday be of use. Most objects can be easily re-obtained if they are actually necessary. A final reason people keep unnecessary objects is because they have a sentimental attachment to them. However, if the object has been forgotten and lost amid a pile of other things, one might ask just how beloved it really is.

Reasons why clients make unnecessary purchases
Often, a client accumulates clutter because he or she has bad shopping habits. Before a client makes any purchase, he or she should consider where the item will be stored. If there is no clear answer, then the item should not be purchased. Clients also get themselves into trouble when they go shopping without having any specific items in mind. Aimless browsing is a great way to accumulate unnecessary possessions. Paradoxically, disorganized people often purchase too much storage equipment. They know they have a problem with organization, and they think that purchasing more and more containers is a good way to solve it. However, simply purchasing containers is not the same thing as developing an organization system. Finally, many clients accumulate too many objects because they have difficulty resisting things that are either

free or on sale. Before acquiring a discounted object, the client needs to consider exactly how he or she will use it.

How collectibles can become clutter
Many of a professional organizer's clients will have large collections of things, like baseball cards, stuffed animals, or coins, to name a few. The client will often believe that he or she should hold onto these items because they will be worth something someday. However, many of these clients have never actually taken the time to learn how collectible items can be converted into money. In most cases, the client is likely to receive far less for his or her collection then he or she may expect. When dealing with collections, a professional organizer should always be sensitive to the client's feelings. Collections are accumulated over a long time, and the client is likely to have a strong sentimental attachment to his or her collectibles. The organizer needs to help the client see the real value of the items in the collection rather than their perceived value, but the organizer should not denigrate the feelings of the client in doing so.

How clutter can contribute to anxiety
To some people, it is crazy to think that piles of paper can lead to chronic anxiety. But this is exactly what happens in the home or office of a disorganized person. When a person is constantly surrounded by objects that need to be put away, repaired, discarded, or processed, he or she is constantly reminded of work that needs to be done. When a person is constantly reminded of work that needs to be done but that he or she is not doing, the person becomes anxious. People love to own things, but they never realize how these things come to own them by occupying their time, attention, and care. Starting now and developing a solid organization system is a great way to eliminate anxiety and create peace in the home or office. A person who is surrounded by clutter spends his or her time thinking about the future instead of living in the present.

How clutter can create more work for people over time than an organization project
Many people feel like they don't have the time to undertake an organization project, but they don't realize that failing to organize themselves will cost them a great deal more time in the future. When a person leaves piles of clutter around, he or she is constantly devoting tiny amounts of time and attention to plans for removing it. This is a steady drain on the person's energy, creativity, and productivity. Moreover, having more objects simply means having more objects to clean, so housekeeping tasks are always more of a challenge for disorganized people. When a person has too many things, he or she is likely to forget where things are, which creates another level of anxiety and confusion. Sadly, for many people, clutter and work increase continuously in a self-reinforcing cycle. The only way to break this cycle is to get organized once and for all.

Techniques for reducing mental clutter
Professional organizers largely deal with the unnecessary objects that accumulate in physical spaces, but they should also be aware that physical clutter is almost always mirrored by mental clutter. Clients will often need to learn some techniques for clearing their mental space so that they can think straight. Perhaps the best way to clear the mind is exercise. Another useful technique is to get a spiral notebook and free write. When free writing, the client should not edit his or her expression at all. Instead, the client should simply allow whatever comes out of his or her pen to emerge. Making a list is another great way to reduce mental clutter. The client should list all of the tasks he or she needs to accomplish, and then use this list as an external memory

so that his or her brain can concentrate on more important matters.

Excuses people make for avoiding organization projects

A professional organizer will hear many reasons why the present is a bad time to start an organization project. One common refrain is that there is simply too much to do and the client doesn't know where to start. The best way to get over this feeling of being overwhelmed is simply to do something. Too often, clients focus on the ideal state for their room or office and allow this to keep them from making any progress at all. Just because the room has not obtained perfection does not mean it is not better than it was before. When the client doesn't know where to start, the organizer needs to encourage him or her to just start somewhere. Moreover, the client should be encouraged to focus exclusively on one single area and not diffuse his or her emphasis at the beginning of a project. The organizer should help the client focus on the immediate task to avoid being stymied by long-term thoughts.

Describe how procrastination is tied to disorganization.

Almost all of the clients that a professional organizer deals with will be procrastinators of one sort or another. That is, they put off unpleasant tasks. The problem with procrastination is that the task still needs to be accomplished, and the procrastinator has made himself more anxious in the interim. One of the best ways to tackle procrastination is to get in the habit of doing the hardest task first. Typically, a person will have the most energy and motivation at the beginning, so this can be applied to whatever is likely to be the most recalcitrant job. Once this is done, the client will feel a sense of momentum that can carry them through the rest of the job. A professional

organizer needs to hold clients accountable for their procrastination, or else this bad habit will eat away at whatever progress is made during the project.

Activities an organizer might request a client to perform before beginning a project

In the time between the initial assessment and the beginning of a project, many professional organizers will give clients a brief "homework" assignment. This is especially useful when a client appears overwhelmed by his or her problems and uncertain of how to begin solving them. One useful task for a client to perform is to take a series of pictures of the problem area. Another valuable task would be to identify some local charities that would be interested in the donation of unwanted items. Many clients need to spend time thinking about their overall goals for the project. It is common for clients to recognize that they have a problem, but to not be able to see the best solution. A very general homework assignment is to have the client keep a journal about the organizing process. In the journal, the client could record his or her ideas, hopes, and even doubts about the project as it begins.

Fears a client may have before starting an organization project

Clients will often be a little afraid before beginning an organization project, but the reason for this fear may be surprising to the novice organizer. For many clients, staying disorganized is a way of avoiding high expectations and possible disappointment. The client may unconsciously be keeping himself disorganized so that it will be impossible for him or her to be expected to do more. The client may be secretly afraid of failing to meet the high expectations that would be created if he or she were seen as more efficient. The confidence to succeed is something a professional organizer must cultivate in the client. Clients should not be allowed to avoid their potential. Instead, the organizer should build client confidence by setting and attaining goals and shifting the client's focus from long-term anxieties to immediate tasks. Often, clients who are secretly afraid of success spend too much time thinking about the future and fail to take the necessary steps to make that future a positive one.

How perfectionism can interfere with organization projects

It is common in organization projects for a client to become excessively concerned with perfecting a room. As the saying has it, these clients make the perfect enemy of the good because they discount any solution that offers improvements rather than immediate flawlessness. The result is inaction and a slow decline. A professional organizer should encourage clients to try different strategies and not feel as if they have to make the perfect decision every time. Indeed, an organizer should help the client see that all solutions are provisional and therefore subject to refinement and improvement. The professional organizer's focus should always be on continuous progress and improvement, not perfection. Life is a messy affair, and clients should not be given the expectation that a professional organizer will be able to create perfect systems for them. Instead, the organizer should indicate that constant maintenance will be a part of the system.

Organizational problems

Mechanical in nature
An organizational problem can be described as mechanical in nature when it is based on broken or inefficient objects. For instance, if a client has a beautiful roll top desk with drawers that do not fully open, resulting in a pile of paper on the desktop, then the client has a mechanical problem. If the client has to lean all of his weight against a door in order to set the bolt, he has a mechanical problem. In a way, mechanical organizational problems are the easiest to fix: they simply require a toolbox and a little manual effort. However, there may be some underlying psychological problems for a client who persistently adapts to broken and inefficient machines rather than fixing them. These irritating little hassles wear away at a person's psyche, and resigning oneself to living with them rather than taking the time to fix them is a sign of depression for some people. For many people, though, mechanical problems are a mystery, and a little bit of skill applied by the professional organizer can make a huge difference almost immediately.

Emotional in nature
Some organizational problems are rooted in the client's emotions. This is perhaps most commonly true of situations in which the client is unable to throw away or store items that have a sentimental value. A professional organizer never wants to encourage a client to discard beloved items, but the organizer may suggest that the client find a better place for unused memorabilia that is filling valuable space in an area of high activity. Most clients will have some sort of storage area in their house where valued possessions can be preserved. Even when a client is well aware that he or she is never going to use the object again, he or she will be unable to part with it. It is not the job of the organizer to convince the client otherwise, but rather to show that the object can be kept nearby without allowing it to interfere with life as it is presently lived.

Situational in nature
Some organizational problems are rooted in particular situations, meaning that a recent life event or crisis has jumbled the client's world. This may be a negative

event, like a divorce or a death in the family, or a joyful one, like the birth of a new child. One of the most important aspects of the assessment phase is determining whether the client has experienced any great change in his or her personal life recently. In most cases, clients will be aware of how these significant life events have affected their organization. However, and especially in extremely negative circumstances, a client's perception may be clouded. Of course, it is not the job of the professional organizer to resolve the client's personal issues. If necessary, the professional organizer should refer the client to a mental health specialist or other professional. However, the professional organizer can still improve the client's life so long as he or she understands the situation. When a client is in a transition period, it may be necessary for the organizer to set up systems that are not meant to be permanent. If the client's organizational problems are situational, then the professional organizer must take special care to ensure that the emotional as well as the physical needs of the client are being met.

Systemic in nature

Some organizational problems are systemic in nature, meaning that the client has created an inefficient process for living and/or working in a particular space. Professional organizers should remember that not everyone shares their intuition for efficiency and simplicity. The professional organizer will be astonished at some of the cumbersome and overly elaborate systems clients have devised. Some professional organizers feel that dealing with systemic problems is their most satisfying work because clients are so relieved and grateful to be shown an easier way. One way to determine whether a client's problems are systemic in nature is to isolate the various steps in a process and then determine whether each of these steps is absolutely

necessary. In many cases, a little investigation will show that the client is habitually performing actions that are redundant, ineffective, or irrelevant.

How guilt can contribute to disorganization

Some clients accumulate clutter because they feel guilty about discarding anything that might have some value. It is the job of the professional organizer to remind the client that it is not important for an object to have value, but for it to have value *for the client*. Guilt-related hoarding is especially common when a client has inherited the possessions of a deceased family member. For instance, many clients cannot bear to discard any of their deceased mother or father's things because to do so would reopen the grief associated with that parent's death. The organizer should be respectful of these feelings and try to help the client work through them at his or her pace. The organizer may encourage the client to retain a few special items while discarding the rest. It can be very therapeutic for a client to donate the possessions of a deceased loved one to charity so that they can continue to be appreciated.

Ethical and practical issues related to taking before-and-after pictures during the assessment phase of an organization project

One of the cornerstones of marketing for professional organizers is before-and-after pictures. This is with good reason: before-and-after pictures provide a dramatic image of the almost miraculous changes that a professional organizer can accomplish. However, some clients may be uncomfortable with having their living or working space photographed before it has been improved. Clients may be embarrassed about their amount of clutter or about particular items on display. The professional organizer must always obtain permission from the client before using photographs for marketing purposes. The organizer will need to take pictures during an initial visit out of necessity, but these pictures should remain confidential unless the client has given his or her explicit consent. In many cases, clients who would be uneasy about releasing photos at the beginning of the project are so pleased with the results of the work that they are excited about sharing before-and-after pictures with the world. It is a good idea for a professional organizer to have a formal consent form, however, so that clients cannot say photographs were taken and used against their will.

Rate of pay

Many starting professional organizers struggle to establish a rate of pay that is sustainable for them and fair for the customer. For many people, asking for a certain amount of money is an awkward and embarrassing process. Even those beginning organizers who feel very confident of their skills may feel sheepish about asking for money to perform tasks at which they have very little experience. Nevertheless, every professional organizer needs to determine a fair rate. A number of factors contribute to this calculation. These include the organizer's experience, the region of the country, and the rates charged by local competitors. A professional organizer should always do some research before establishing rates. Also, it is important to note that rates are not inflexible; a professional organizer may charge different rates for customers of different means. Most professional organizers have different rates for individual and corporate clients. Finally, a professional organizer can always adjust his or her rates once operations have begun.

<u>Discussing rates</u>
For many beginning professional organizers, the most difficult part of an initial conversation with a client is the discussion of rates. Many people feel awkward requesting money. Beginning professional organizers may be scared that the client will react very negatively to a proposed rate of pay. One way to resolve this anxiety is to create a specific script for discussing payment with clients. The script can then be practiced on friends, family, and other professionals. This activity will help the organizer get more comfortable discussing the subject, and will give him or her feedback about specific language. When discussing payment, an organizer needs to convey the confidence that he or she is worth the quoted rate. Of course, the organizer also needs to support this confidence with performance.

There is some debate in the world of professional organization as to whether clients should be billed for an initial assessment. Most industry leaders, however, recommend that the client be billed at the normal rate for this visit. When the client is paying, the professional organizer feels more obligated to do a thorough and complete assessment. Also, the professional organizer will make all sorts of helpful comments during the course of the assessment, and it is only fair that he or she be compensated for this expertise. A professional organizer does not want to feel reticent about sharing tips just because the client is not currently being billed. Another problem with not billing clients for an initial assessment is that it encourages people to solicit an appraisal without really being serious about obtaining services. The best formula is for a professional organizer to always give his or her best effort and always expect compensation for it.

Billing for travel time

In most cases, a professional organizer will not bill clients for travel time unless the distance between the organizer's office and the job site is significant. Depending on the region of the country, a significant amount of travel time may be anywhere from half an hour to an hour and a half. Some professional organizers bill their clients for any travel time over a certain amount. For instance, the organizer might say that the client is liable for any travel time in excess of one hour. The client may decide that it is better to find another professional organizer who is based nearby. If so, the professional organizer can help with the referral. So long as the organizer always acts in the best interest of the client, he or she will reap benefits in the future.

Risks of setting rates too high or low

Establishing rates is one of the trickiest issues for a beginning professional organizer. There is a temptation to set rates very low, either to generate some initial business or because the organizer is not yet confident in his or her abilities. This should be avoided, however, for a couple of reasons. For one thing, many clients will be skeptical of a professional whose rates are far below those of competitors. The client may perceive that the organizer is unskilled or inferior in quality. Also, professional organizers who establish rates far below market value may find themselves locked into this pricing scale even as their experience and earning potential increase. It is far better to establish market-level rates and allow business to build slowly. Of course, if an organizer sets his or her rates too high, clients will be reluctant to hire him or her. The general range for beginning professional organizers working with private clients is between $50 and $150 per hour.

Risks of overcharging clients for small expenses

During the completion of a project, a professional organizer will likely use plenty of supplies and equipment. Without thinking about it, some professional organizers itemize all of the products used and add them to the client's bill. It is much better to set a higher initial hourly rate that includes the costs of supplies and equipment. If the client receives a bill on which many small charges are listed, he or she may become resentful. The organizer obviously deserves to be reimbursed for the cost of the products he or she stocks, but this cost should be considered as part of the general service provided, not as a separate expense. This directive does not apply to overtime, however. The professional organizer should always bill clients for the total amount of time spent on the project, even if this is slightly in excess of the estimate provided during the assessment phase. When a professional organizer determines that it will be necessary to work extra hours, he or she should disclose this information to the client.

Establishing package rates

Some professional organizers have found that they can generate extra business when they offer clients package rates. That is, they give the client a special lower rate in exchange for prompt payment at the beginning of the project. For instance, the client might receive a 15 percent discount if he or she commits to at least 20 hours of service. This arrangement has advantages for the professional organizer because it guarantees business and allows the organizer to set his or her schedule ahead of time. Many of a professional organizer's clients will be affluent, so it may not be a problem for them to write a large check before any services have been provided. Of course, professional organizers who offer package deals must make sure that their services justify the payment. If an organizer feels that being paid ahead of time will sap his or her motivation, he or she should not offer package deals.

Advantages and disadvantages of offering project rather than hourly rates
When a client has a particularly large or complex organization problem, he or she may be reluctant to contact a professional organizer out of fear that the number of hours required will balloon the expense. There is a temptation, then, for the organizer to establish a fixed rate for the project to allay the client's concerns. In general, however, this is a bad idea, especially for the beginning professional organizer. It is just too difficult to predict how a project will unfold. Even experienced professional organizers are constantly surprised by the unforeseen problems (or solutions) they discover once they have begun their work in earnest. For this reason, it is much more sensible to charge a client by the hour. The professional organizer might be concerned that establishing a project rate will result in unpaid labor, but it can be equally embarrassing to establish a high project rate and then finish the assignment much quicker than expected.

Value of establishing a special rate for friends and family
Some professional organizers elect to establish a special lower rate for their friends and family. This can be a great thing, so long as the organizer does not provide most of his or her services at this rate, and so long as good boundaries between personal and professional life are maintained. It is a joy to help loved ones get their lives in order, but the professional organizer needs to maintain his or her professional status at the same time. Friends and family should not make requests that a normal client would not. By charging loved ones only slightly less than his or her usual rate, the professional organizer signifies that the

relationship is special but that the "client" is not taking advantage of him or her. For a beginning professional organizer, providing service for family and friends is a fantastic way to build experience, generate word-of-mouth, and create a marketing portfolio.

Action Plan Development

Planning phase of an organization project

The completion of the assessment phase does not mean that the professional organizer will cease to collect information about the client. Indeed, client assessment can be said to go on throughout the project. However, once the professional organizer believes that he or she has a solid grasp of the client's problems, strengths, and desires, it is time to move on to the second phase: planning. A successful plan will be aligned with the client's desires and expectations. It will retain all of the things the client likes about the space as it is currently organized while eliminating all of those things that create frustration and inefficiency. A plan must be more complicated than just removing clutter. It must also indicate new possibilities for the space. It is not necessary for a plan to be complete at first, but it must be detailed enough for the organizer and client to begin implementation. There must be a constant and productive dialogue between the organizer and client during the planning phase, or else there is the possibility that plans will become sidetracked.

Importance of providing a time estimate
When devising a plan for an organization project, the professional organizer is obliged to give the client some idea of how long implementation will take. This is necessarily an inexact science, but an experienced organizer will develop a good sense of how long certain processes take and to what extent certain types of clients will expand or contract the project. For instance, clients who want to be intimately involved with every detail of the project may be a joy to work with, but will most likely extend the duration of the project. By contrast, clients who give the professional organizer plenty of leeway in which to work tend to see their projects completed more quickly, though they may be surprised or disappointed by the results. A professional organizer needs to have performed a comprehensive assessment of both the client and physical space in order to provide an accurate timetable. It is much better to estimate a longer time and then complete the project early than it is to make unrealistic promises that will inevitably be broken.

Time required for some basic organizational projects
A professional organizer needs to be able to give the client a general idea of how long the project will take. However, for a beginning organizer, it may be difficult to calculate the size of the project, the amount of time available, and the personal characteristics of the client. Beginning organizers should be aware of some rough duration estimates for common projects. For instance, organizing a closet usually takes between four and eight hours. Naturally, as with all these estimates, the actual duration is dependent on the desires of the client, the amount of space, and the amount of clutter. A bedroom of average size will typically take between eight and 12 hours to organize. A garage will usually take about the same amount of time. Kitchens, on the other hand, are notoriously complicated, and are likely to take between 10 and 14 hours on average to organize. Organizing an office, when the project includes redesigning the filing system, may take as little as 16 hours or as many as 24. These rough figures can serve as a general point of orientation for a beginning professional organizer.

Extent to which a professional organizer should sell potential clients on his or her services

There is some debate among professional organizers about whether it is appropriate to aggressively pursue potential clients. Some professionals feel comfortable with using elements of persuasion in order to obtain business, while others feel that it is important to let the client come to a decision on his or her own. The extent to which a professional organizer engages in salesmanship may vary, but the important thing is that the organizer never deviates from the truth when making his or her case to potential clients. One way to ensure that clients will feel deceived is to make unrealistic promises or quote artificially low rates. A professional organizer can make an amazing difference in the lives of his or her clients, but he or she is not a miracle worker. Of course, the organizer needs to represent his or her business well in order to attract clients, but this should never cross over into fraud or half-truths. The client should always be given a fair opportunity to decide whether professional organizational services are right for him or her.

How client behavior can expand the duration of a project

When estimating the length of time that will be required for a project, there is a temptation for the organizer to consider how long the work would take if he or she were working in isolation. However, the organizer must always take into account the presence of the client. In most cases, the client's behavior will add time to the project. This is not because clients are willfully inefficient or dilatory, but because it often takes them a while to arrive at a full understanding of their problem and the work required to solve it. A professional organizer cannot force the client to understand his or her problem; this process needs to occur at its own pace. Many people with organization

problems are naturally indecisive, which adds time to the project. To be safe, an organizer should always estimate how long it would take him or her to finish a project alone, and then add 20 to 30 percent to that estimate to account for the client.

How organization projects are interconnected

When creating a time estimate for an organization project, a professional organizer should remember that solving problems in one space usually requires expanding the work into others. For instance, helping a client clean out a cluttered garage may lead to overcrowding in other storage spaces, like attics or basements. It is important that the organizer's work not leave behind problems in secondary areas. The organizer must account for the inevitability of the project's expansion. In addition, the organizer should explain to the client that their work together is likely to run into unforeseen places. In order for an organizer to leave behind a comprehensive system, he or she needs to address all of the consequences of the original project's completion. The time estimate should account for this.

How a beginning professional organizer should handle an overwhelming project

It is inevitable that a new professional organizer will eventually feel overwhelmed by the scope or complexity of a project. A professional must learn to recognize when this occurs and how to obtain help. Professional organizers should never feel embarrassed or reticent to call upon colleagues when necessary. Some organization projects require a team of professionals. In some cases, the objects that need to be moved will be too heavy for the organizer, who will need to enlist the services of some stronger people. In other cases, the professional organizer will recognize that the client requires a different approach than he or

- 57 -

she can provide. There's no shame in recognizing a need for help; the only unforgivable sin as a professional is to persevere with a task for which one is knowingly unqualified. This is yet another scenario in which it will pay to have served as an apprentice or studied with a more experienced organizer. When feeling overwhelmed, a beginning professional organizer should be able to call upon senior people in the industry for guidance.

Extent to which you should guarantee success to the client
A professional organizer should be confident in his or her abilities, but should stop short of issuing ironclad guarantees to clients. There are simply too many variables outside of the organizer's control for a guarantee to be possible. For instance, if the client is unwilling to change his or her habits and commit to the new organization system, the project is doomed through no fault of the organizer. If an unforeseen event throws the client's life into chaos during the project, the organizer cannot be blamed. An organizer can always guarantee his or her best effort and full attention, but cannot guarantee that the shared work will produce permanent positive changes for the client. To some extent, an organizer can guarantee satisfaction provided that the client is committed to the process. This guarantee is easier to fulfill when the organizer is constantly assessing the project and maintaining good communication with the client.

Creating a project schedule
After the client has agreed to obtain services, the organizer should try to establish a schedule for the project. It is a good idea to schedule the next meeting as soon as possible to build on the momentum from the assessment. Whenever possible, the organizer should try to schedule work sessions for the same time every week. This creates a sense of habit that reinforces the client's commitment to the project. Once the schedule is established, most professional organizers do not call to confirm appointments. The organizer's time is too valuable to waste on reiterating agreements that have already been made. The client should be aware that once an appointment has been set, he or she will not be reminded of it. One other reason to avoid confirming appointments ahead of time is that it encourages clients to cancel them. When the client is required to take the initiative in order to cancel appointments, he or she is less likely to do so. Most professional organizers also have a strict policy about cancellations. It is typical for an organizer to charge the client a certain percentage of the hourly fee if an appointment is canceled with insufficient notice. For instance, an organizer might charge the client half the fee for the scheduled visit if it is canceled less than 48 hours ahead of time.

Degree to which an organizing project plan should be flexible
Especially at the beginning of a project, the plan agreed upon by the professional organizer and client should remain flexible. It is common for clients to change their opinions and emphasis in between the assessment and the first work session. For instance, the client may have realized that the organization problems in his or her bedroom closet are rooted in an inefficient system for laundry, which he or she now wants to tackle first. The organizer should be accommodating to these changes of heart. After all, organization projects are inherently interconnected, and so it is likely that the organizer would eventually address all of these issues anyway. So long as the overall goals are kept in mind, it should not matter particularly where the project begins. In some cases, the organizer may disagree with the client's desire to shift the initial focus of the project. If the

organizer can argue his or her side in a respectful way, that is fine. The client may be persuaded or may insist on his or her preference, in which case the organizer should accede.

Importance of the client's commitment to the organization process

Many beginning organizers feel that any client is better than none, but an experienced professional will assert that finding the right clients is the only way to establish a successful long-term business. If clients are not truly ready to commit to the project, they will make the organizer's life miserable. An organizer wants clients who have sought him or her out, not those who have been coerced. This is one reason why it is important to ask potential clients how they heard about professional organization services. If the client says that he or she was forced to make the call by a spouse or boss, the organizer can expect a lot more friction during the course of the project. Many professional organizers don't offer gift certificates because they don't want to work with clients who may not want their help. Some people might even be offended by the gift of professional organizational services and might take this insult out on the organizer. It can be frustrating for a beginning professional organizer to wait for clients, but the reward of isolating good clients is well worth it.

Action Plan Implementation and Project Management

Initial steps of the implementation phase of an organization project

After constructing as detailed and comprehensive a plan as possible, the professional organizer will begin to implement it. In a typical project, the first step is to remove all of the items from storage. For instance, in a kitchen project, all of the drawers and cabinets should be emptied of their contents. After all the miscellaneous items in the room are out of storage, they should be grouped together according to their characteristics. That is, all of the knives should go together, all of the silverware should go together, all of the coffee mugs should go together, and so on. This is not yet the time to discard objects or to make any permanent decisions about their placement. The only intention of this process is to sort objects into sensible groups. A beginning professional organizer may be shocked at the amount of disorganization revealed by this simple process. Often, the uselessness or triviality of certain objects is revealed by the category into which they are placed. Some objects will seem to belong to more than one group. In this case, the client should make the call.

Items needed on the job site

Professional organizers will need a basic kit of tools and supplies for every job. There are certain essential items that each kit must contain. For instance, a professional organizer needs to have a camera. It is best to have a digital camera with a spare memory card so that there is no limit to the number of pictures that can be taken. A professional organizer should also bring a selection of pens, pencils, and black markers. The kit should also include scissors, a calculator, a stapler, post-it notes, a letter opener, and tape measures. The professional organizer should have a set of white labels and colored dot stickers for categorizing file folders at all times. A professional organizer should also have a set of small index cards and envelopes. Some organizers elect to bring a label maker, which necessitates a set of replacement tapes. It is also a good idea for the organizer to have both graph and notebook paper. Finally, a professional organizer should have a wide variety of file folders and hanging files.

Type of bag a that should be brought to the job site

A professional organizer must bring along a variety of tools and equipment, so it is important for him or her to have a large bag. The professional organizer's bag does not have to be elaborate or fancy, but it should have many different compartments. The best way to identify the appropriate type of bag is to make a list of all the items that must be brought to the job site and find the bag that best accommodates all these items. Some professional organizers elect to carry two different bags: one for strictly professional items, and one for personal items, like wallet and keys. Every professional organizer will develop a different system. The important thing for a professional is to find the bag that will keep him or her organized so that no time is wasted on the job site.

Appropriate clothing for the various phases of a project

A professional organizer needs to convey personal control in every aspect of his or her life, including clothing. The appropriate clothing for a professional will depend upon the activity. During an initial meeting with the client, it is appropriate to wear business casual attire, like slacks or a skirt and a nice shirt or blouse. When the project begins, however, the organizer will want to wear something more durable and comfortable. Most professional organizers have a closet full of jeans and khakis. It is a good idea to have dark-colored clothing so that stains are less visible. The professional organizer's clothing should not be too nice or ostentatious during a project, or else either the organizer or client will feel reticent about getting dirty. When working with corporate clients, the professional organizer should inquire about the dress code in advance. Besides plenty of work clothes, a professional organizer will need to have some nicer apparel for meetings, marketing calls, and networking events.

Types of shoes, hair, and makeup that are appropriate for professional organizers

While engaged in a project, a professional organizer must wear shoes that are comfortable and supportive. Most professional organizers select broken-in running shoes or a comfortable pair of black or brown flats. If the organizer wears sneakers, they must be clean. A professional organizer should never wear sandals or open-toed shoes while on the job. As for other aspects of appearance, a professional organizer should adopt a conservative, low-maintenance haircut. Hair should always be kept out of the face so that the organizer does not need to be constantly brushing it behind his or her ear. With regard to jewelry, a professional organizer should only wear a few tasteful items. A professional organizer does not want to wear long, dangling earrings or necklaces that will interfere with his or her work.

First working session

The first working session with a new client should be scheduled as soon after the assessment as possible. It is always a good idea to arrive at the client's home or office a little early in order to start work precisely on time. The first order of business for this work session will be briefly reviewing the project plan. Specifically, the organizer wants to discuss the activities that will be performed during the initial session. A client may be startled or even offended if an organizer begins sifting through his or her possessions without warning or pretense. Even if the general goals of the project have already been articulated, it is polite for the organizer to briefly restate them for the client. After the plan has been discussed and agreed upon, the organizer and client should settle into work. It is good for this initial work session to be as long as possible so that enough progress can be made that the client will want to avoid backsliding. At the minimum, an initial work session should last four hours. The organizer should leave at least half an hour at the end of the session for cleaning any messes and advising the client as to how to maintain the progress that has been made so far.

<u>Importance of making clear progress</u>
It is important for the professional organizer to solidify the client's commitment by producing some tangible results during the first working session. Of course, every working session with a professional organizer should produce results, but this is especially true of the first session when the client's participation may still be variable. It is better to accomplish a smaller task fully during the first session than to leave a larger task incomplete. If the organizer can leave the client's home or office having effectively implemented one small new organization system, the client will

be reminded of the value of organization services continually until the next session. Progress made during this first session should be perceptible, but it should also be stated explicitly by the organizer. That is, at the end of the first work session, the organizer should review with the client exactly what they have accomplished together. Sometimes, a client will participate in the work of organizing but will not fully understand why they are doing what they are doing. It is particularly important at the beginning of a project for the organizer to educate the client.

Handling an unexpected emotional reaction by a client

An organization project involves sorting through a client's personal possessions, which can sometimes provoke an unexpected emotional response. For instance, a client might unearth some old family photographs that evoke nostalgia or remembrance of a tragic loss. When this occurs, the last thing the organizer should do is ignore the client's feelings. At the same time, a professional organizer should not endeavor to provide psychological services for which he or she is not trained. The best response to an emotional episode is to acknowledge the client's feelings, show respect for them, and suggest a pause in the work. The organizer may ask the client if he or she would like to share, but by no means should the organizer insist. The organizer will not be able to have an honest relationship with the client if emotional responses are not acknowledged. The client should not be made to feel that this is an unusual occurrence because the process of organizing possessions often awakens the dormant issues in the client's life. It is always good to reiterate that organizing is an external process that can have marked benefits on the client's internal state.

Responding to clients who become resistant and angry

Sometimes, a client who seemed committed to the project during the assessment and planning phases suddenly becomes resistant or even angry once work begins. Many clients have fantasized about tackling their organization problems, but shy away from the project as it begins. It is important for a professional organizer to be patient. When faced with a resistant client, the organizer should reiterate the goals of the project and the necessity of starting somewhere. If the client remains resistant, the organizer may suggest a brief timeout. In most cases, the client will work through his or her reservations and agree to continue the work within a few minutes. However, it is possible that a client will suddenly decide to terminate the project. An organizer should never force a client to do anything against his or her will. Of course, the organizer will need to bill the client for the services rendered, and most organizers will include the full cost of the truncated work session. As much as possible, though, the organizer should seek to understand, validate, and adapt to the client's chaotic emotions.

Many beginning professional organizers are surprised or shocked when a client suddenly begins to express anger during the project. It is rare, though, that this anger is the result of an error or a lack of courtesy by the professional. Organizers should be aware of the aspects of a project that are likely to trigger an angry response by the client. Perhaps the most common reason for anger is a defensive response. Clients may feel embarrassed by their possessions or their lack of organization, and then they lash out at a person who they perceive as judging them. It is important for the organizer to allay these concerns by reassuring the client that his or her problems are not that unusual (even if they are). A client might also become angry if they realize

Copyright © Mometrix Media. You have been licensed one copy of this document for personal use only. Any other reproduction or redistribution is strictly prohibited. All rights reserved.

that they would rather be doing something else or if they regret having arranged the project. Again, it is important in such a scenario for the organizer to reiterate the positive consequences of completing the project. As with all of the client's emotional responses, it is important for the organizer to acknowledge and validate anger.

It is important for an organizer not to ignore a client's anger. Instead, the organizer needs to find a constructive way to resolve the issues underlying this emotional response. The easiest way to handle a client's angry outburst is to suggest a brief timeout so that everyone can calm themselves. Another approach is to tackle a different aspect of the project. A client is more likely to become angry when beginning an especially large or complex part of the project, so it can be therapeutic to shift attention to something easy. If the client becomes belligerent, the organizer needs to intervene and reestablish professional decorum. An organizer should be tolerant of the client's emotional response to the process, but should not have to deal with disrespectful behavior. It is important, however, to be aware that only rarely is an angry or aggressive response actually directed at the organizer. In most cases, the client's anger is really directed inward.

Importance of appropriately scheduling tasks

Some of the steps in an organization project will require a minimum of several hours to accomplish. For instance, when organizing the kitchen, one of the first steps is to remove and sort everything from the drawers and cabinets. This is not a task that can be accomplished in less than two or three hours, so the professional organizer must make sure that there is adequate time to finish it before initiating. Even though clients are

in the middle of an organization project, they still need to be using their living and working space while the project is ongoing. The client cannot continue to use his or her kitchen with every object on the counter until the professional organizer returns for their next meeting. An experienced professional organizer will anticipate the steps in a process that require large blocks of time and will make sure that the client is aware of this necessity as well. In some cases, it may be useful to divide a large step in the project into multiple smaller steps to accommodate the schedule of the organizer or client.

Process of disposing of objects

After all of the objects in the targeted physical space have been removed from storage and sorted, the professional organizer and client can begin to identify those objects that may be discarded. Anything that is broken, never used, irrelevant, old, or disliked is a candidate for elimination. If a client likes an object but is not using it, it should be relocated. If the client would use the object were it not broken, it should be fixed. Sometimes, the client and the professional organizer will be able to eliminate entire categories of objects from a space. In other cases, the sorting process will reveal that there are too many of a particular type of object, and that some of these items may be discarded. For instance, many people tend to compile massive numbers of coffee mugs over the years. Grouping all of these mugs on the kitchen counter can demonstrate to the client that it is not necessary to keep all of them.

Basic system for discarding objects

The objects a client agrees to discard may be removed to several different locations. Some objects will not actually be given away, but rather will be relocated to another place in the home or office. Some objects will be so obsolete, broken, or valueless that they must be simply thrown away. However, many of the unwanted objects in a client's home or office could still have value to someone else, so they should be placed in a box for donation. A professional organizer should be familiar with all of the charitable organizations, as for instance Goodwill and the Salvation Army, that collect unwanted goods. In many cases, these organizations will even accept unwieldy items, like large appliances and pieces of furniture, which saves the organizer and client labor. Also, the donation of some large items may create a possibility of tax deduction for the client. At this point in the reorganization project, however, it is not necessary to follow through on any of these plans; instead, the organizer should focus on placing the unwanted items into various boxes and setting them aside.

Putting objects away

After all of the objects in the targeted space have been collected and categorized, and unwanted objects have been discarded, the professional organizer and client will begin to put the wanted objects away. It is important to take a fresh approach to each object: that is, the professional organizer and client should strive to find the perfect place for each object and should not just put things away where convenient or where they have gone in the past. Items should be kept together in the groups made during the sorting phase. So, in the kitchen, all of the items associated with grilling should be kept in the same place. In the bedroom, all of the client's swimwear should be kept together. It is still possible and even useful for the client to discard items during this phase of the project. Sometimes, it is not until a client tries to find a place for an object that he or she realizes the object has no place. The professional organizer should be careful to note to the client that putting away

objects does not represent the end of the organization project.

Quest for appropriate storage

After a client's objects have been gathered, organized, streamlined, and put away, the organizer will turn his or her attention to storage. For many organizers, this is the best part of any project. Professional organizers need to have an extensive collection of sources for storage materials. They should receive relevant catalogs, and should be intimately familiar with the inventory of storage stores in the area. However, in some cases it is not necessary to acquire any new storage objects. Some clients already own plenty of containers, files, and bins, but simply have not yet put these objects to their proper use. It is often a good idea to use the client's existing storage containers as temporary solutions while more appropriate or better storage is being acquired. This will give the client a taste of the dramatic life improvements he or she is about to experience. Even using a cardboard box or paper bag as a temporary storage can help the client visualize the final results of the project. In some cases, the use of temporary storage will illuminate new information about how the client uses his or her space.

How clients should handle unwanted gifts

Everyone receives gifts that he or she does not want to keep. Too often, however, a disorganized person hangs onto these gifts out of a feeling of obligation. A professional organizer should give clients a strategy for handling this problem. Obviously, the client should thank the gift giver, but then the client should understand that it is his or her decision what to do with the gift. The client may pass the gift along to a person who is more likely to appreciate it, or may donate the gift to charity. In most cases, the person who gave the gift would be glad to know that it went somewhere that it could be loved and used, rather than becoming a source of anxiety and guilt for the recipient. Disposing of unwanted gifts should always be done with tact, but it should not be avoided because it is a problem that every person must face at some point.

How hand-me-downs can become a source of clutter

Many parents like to keep clothing and toys around so that they can be used by more than one child. This makes sense in most cases, but only if the items can be efficiently stored without detracting from the home. People rarely consider the costs of storing items for several years. In some cases, it just makes more sense to repurchase the item when the younger child needs it. Items should always be stored in such a way that they will be in good condition when they are needed again. The client should never expect that he or she will remember where all of the items are, or indeed what items have been stored. It is a good idea to put labels on all the storage containers and create a master list so that items can be easily found. It is also wise to sort items according to age group.

Necessity of having accessible, labeled storage containers

The storage containers a client uses should be labeled on all sides so that the contents are apparent no matter how the container is stowed. Indeed, many professional organizers recommend that clients obtain clear storage containers so that the contents are visible from the outside. Storage containers that are likely to be used more than once should have clear packing tape affixed to each side, and the tape should be labeled with a black marker. It is always important to purchase an appropriately-sized

container. The organizer and client should measure the space where the container will be placed before purchasing. Also, clients should be aware that some containers are likely to take on more items over time. For instance, if a client purchases a container to hold old photographs, he or she may assume that more photographs will be obtained in the future. Therefore, it is a good idea to purchase a slightly larger container than is necessary at present.

Where clients should store multiple and overflow items

Some clients like to purchase items in bulk, usually because they are able to obtain a discount by doing so. However, buying more products than one currently needs creates obvious storage problems. Clients who are in the habit of buying in bulk should designate a particular place for storing excess items. This overflow storage area can become the "refill station" for the rest of the house. If the client is extremely devoted to purchasing multiple items, he or she should place all of the kitchen items together, all of the bathroom items together, and so on. Items that need to be replaced frequently, like toilet paper, should be kept near the site of use. Other items that have been bought in bulk may be kept where there is available storage space.

Strategies for organizing an entryway

Many clients have difficulty keeping their entryway organized, usually because the members of their family drop whatever they are holding as soon as they enter the house. One way to handle this problem is to designate a certain area in the foyer for each member of the family. There should also be a place for umbrellas and tote bags that are used frequently. For instance, clients who are members of a gym might want to keep their athletic bag near the door. It is also a good idea to have a few hangers in the entryway for keeping extra keys, cell phone equipment, and a small pouch for mail. As much as possible, clients want to keep all of this clutter off of tables and the floor. Some clients find it is useful to place an armoire or chest of drawers in the entryway for the storage of shoes, gloves, hats, and coats.

Creating a makeshift mudroom in the entryway

Many new houses are equipped with a mudroom: a small room with a hard floor where people can take off their shoes and coats. The point of a mudroom is that it does not matter if it gets dirty. When the client doesn't have a mudroom, however, the professional organizer can improvise. One way to do so is by converting a hall closet into a mudroom. First, the closet is emptied out, and then hooks are placed on the inside of the door. Inside the closet, the organizer can place a rack for shoes, mittens, and other accessories. The top shelves of the closet can be used for items that are not currently in season. Another way to improvise a mudroom is to place a wardrobe (or armoire) in the entryway. Hooks can be mounted on the inside of the doors to create additional space for coats. If there is not enough space for a full wardrobe, a smaller chest of drawers could be used.

Kitchen organization

Dividing the kitchen into zones
One easy way to simplify a kitchen is to divide it into zones according to use. For instance, one area of the kitchen can be designated for preparation. This is the place where the basic utensils, knives, cutting boards, and bowls will be kept. It is a good idea to place the preparation area near the sink and the garbage can. Another area of the kitchen could be designated for baking. This would be the place to put the baking sheets, measuring

spoons, wooden spoons, and mixing bowls. Many organizers will also recommend placing all of the ingredients commonly used in baking in this area. These could include shortening, baking soda, baking powder, flour, and brown sugar. A third area of the kitchen could be designated for cooking. It would be a good idea to place this area next to the stove. In the cooking area, there should be easy access to pots, pans, potholders, cookbooks, oils, herbs, and spices. Finally, there could be a storage area for handling leftovers and packaging food for travel. This is the area for paper bags, plastic bags, Tupperware, and aluminum foil.

Placing a message center in the kitchen
In most families, the kitchen is the hub of activity, so it is the perfect place to set up a message center. A message center is a blackboard or dry-erase board where family members can write important information, lists of chores, and important phone numbers. If there is not enough wall space for a message center, space can be created by applying magnetic metallic or blackboard paint to the inside or outside of the cabinet door. If the family would prefer a bulletin board, tiles of cork can be used instead of paint. There should be a space for every family member on the message board. Also, there should be a general rule for clearing the board. For instance, in some families it is commonplace to clear the message board at the end of every week. Information that needs to remain on the message board could be transferred to a more permanent location, such as a list of phone numbers on the refrigerator.

Easy ways to organize pots, pans, and bowls
One of the best ways to keep pots and pans out of the way is to obtain a pot rack. Many cooks have racks that hang from the ceiling. All pots and pans have a ring or a hole at the end of the handle so they can be hung on hooks when they are not in

use or being cleaned. The most convenient place for a pot rack is usually above the stove. To organize large glass bowls, many professional organizers recommend laying a pegboard on the bottom of the drawer. Small pegs are placed in the board and the bowls are laid in between them, so that the bowls do not clank against one another when the drawer is opened. All of the bowls that are used for baking and mixing should be placed in a different area with the rest of the baking equipment. The baking area is also a good place to keep all of the ingredients commonly used in baking, like shortening, brown sugar, baking soda, and baking powder.

Ways to handle appliances and gadgets
Many cooks aspire to use all of their sophisticated kitchen appliances, but find that in practice they really only use a few. To help reduce the clutter on the countertop and cabinets, the cook should choose the gadgets he or she uses consistently and then get rid of the rest. Often, a single appliance can do the work of several. For instance, a food processor can take care of many of the tasks performed by other appliances. Organizers sometimes recommend placing countertop appliances under a decorative box just to remove them from sight. Appliances and gadgets that have too many parts or take too long to clean should be discarded. All of the appliances that are necessary should be kept near their position of use and grouped together. For instance, all of the baking appliances should be kept in the same place.

Strategies for handling Tupperware clutter
Tupperware was invented to make food storage and organization easy, but it can easily get out of control and become a source of major clutter in the kitchen. The first step to organizing Tupperware is to take it all out of the cabinet and make sure that every container has a lid. All of the lids that do not have a container and all of the containers that do not have a lid should be thrown away. Every kitchen needs to have a variety of different Tupperware shapes and sizes, but in most cases there do not need to be multiple versions of the same container. All of the containers can be stored together and the lids can be placed in a lid organizer, which is a tray that affixes to the inside of a cabinet door.

Easy ways to clear space in cabinets
One way to clear space in kitchen cabinets is to stack plates on end instead of on top of one another, because typically there is a great deal of empty space above a stack of plates. It is not too expensive to have a slotted cabinet for plates installed. Another way to utilize the space above the items stored in the cabinet is to install a basket under the shelf. This is a great place to store Tupperware lids, aluminum foil containers, or plastic bags. Organizers often recommend that clients install sliding shelves in their cabinets. A sliding shelf can be pulled out, enabling access to the back of the cabinet. Coffee mugs are a common source of clutter in the kitchen, so many organizers recommend mounting hooks on the underside of the cabinet to hang the mugs on. When evaluating cabinet space, the organizer should always ask the client to consider how often he or she uses certain items. For instance, many clients will keep all of the various sizes of plates in the same cabinet, even if there is one size that they use very rarely.

Maximizing pantry space
If the client has a small pantry, or no pantry at all, this lack of storage space can be remedied in a few different ways. One is to place an armoire in or near the kitchen. These tall pieces of furniture create plenty of room for storage. Another possible solution is to create a "hanging pantry," which is a set of shelves that

hangs over the back of a door. These shelves are usually sturdy enough to support canned foods. Another potential solution is to create a rolling pantry, which is a tall, thin shelving unit mounted on wheels. This set of shelves can be moved all over the kitchen, even into narrow spaces. It is the perfect depth and size for holding items like cereal boxes and canned foods. It can be painted the same color as the kitchen cabinets so that it blends in. When arranging the items in the pantry, the organizer should be sure to place the smaller items, like spices and extracts, at the front so that they do not get lost. Extremely small items, like soup packets and bouillon cubes, should be gathered together in plastic storage containers.

Food organization
Many clients purchase large containers of food which they swiftly find difficult to use. If the container is unwieldy, the client should keep it in the pantry and refill a smaller container for daily use. For instance, the client does not want to get a spoonful of sugar for his or her coffee out of a five-pound bag. In the refrigerator, one way to organize food is to place similar items together. As an example, all the drinks could be placed in the same place, and all the condiments could be placed on the refrigerator door. Some organizers recommend placing all the condiments in a single removable bin so that they can be shifted together onto the counter or table when necessary. Items that are meant to be kept in a cool, dark place, like onions, potatoes, and garlic, should be kept in containers. Onions and garlic should be stored in pantyhose because it keeps the skins from shedding and creating a mess at the bottom of the cabinet or drawer.

Organizing spices
Many people are unaware that spices can expire. Indeed, most spices are really only good for about six months after being opened. Clients should get in the habit of marking the date on spice containers when the seal is broken. An excessive number of spices is a typical problem in a disorganized kitchen. Clients often try to resolve this problem by alphabetizing their spices, but it is much more effective to group them according to use. For instance, all of the spices associated with baking could be placed together. It is also a good idea to place the spices that are used most often at the front of the cabinet. Finding an effective storage container for spices is one of the most challenging projects in many kitchens. One unique solution is to hang a medicine cabinet on the kitchen wall; these cabinets are relatively shallow, so all the spices contained within will be accessible. Another way to store an overflow of spices is to mount a small shelf on the inside of the spice cabinet door.

Basic tools that need to be kept in the kitchen
It is common for kitchens to have an excessive number of tools and gadgets when only a few are essential. For instance, every kitchen needs a good pair of scissors. There are many jobs which are normally performed with a knife, but which can be much more effectively handled with scissors. It is also a good idea to keep a small hammer, a pair of pliers, and a small array of screwdrivers in the kitchen. It is not necessary to have a specific tool box for these items. Instead, the client can place them in a "junk drawer." Every kitchen should only have one junk drawer. This is the place where miscellaneous items and tools are kept. The client should get in the habit of going through his or her junk drawer every six months and removing all of those items that have not been used recently.

Organizing coupons
Many disorganized people amass piles of coupons which eventually costs them more in time and labor than they could

ever save. Whenever possible, coupons should be stored in a place that is convenient to their use. For instance, if the family orders food for takeout and delivery often, they would want to attach restaurant coupons to the associated menus. As for grocery store coupons, these can be stored in a special coupon organizer. Instead of alphabetizing coupons or sorting them by category, clients should get in the habit of sorting them by store. Then the client can simply grab all of the coupons associated with the store to which he or she is heading. More generally, the professional organizer should encourage the client to consider whether clipping coupons is a good investment of his or her time. It can be useful to have the client record how much time he or she is spending collecting coupons and how much money he or she is saving by doing so. Often, clients are surprised to learn just how little coupons are helping them save.

Organizing drawers

One way to bring some order to kitchen drawers is to install special drawer organizers. A drawer organizer is a tray that slides into the drawer and separates its contents. Clients will already be familiar with silverware drawers that separate forks, knives, and spoons. There are drawer organizers for all types of utensils, however, and there are even do-it-yourself kits that allow the organizer and client to customize the kitchen drawers. When kitchen drawers are installed, loose items do not gradually get pushed to the back of the drawer. Also, it becomes possible to store multiple types of items in the same drawer. For instance, a single drawer could contain a set of knives as well as aluminum foil and plastic wrap.

Ways to simplify the garbage system

It is unsightly to have the kitchen garbage can in view, so many organizers will recommend that a client place the can on rails so that it can be wheeled out from a cabinet. If there is enough space, many organizers will install two garbage cans, one of which can be used strictly for perishable items. Often, the can that contains perishable items will be smaller so that the client is encouraged to empty it more frequently. In any case, the garbage can needs to be accessible to people who are working in the kitchen. Placing the can on rails is convenient because it can be wheeled out during periods of intense work when a great deal of garbage is being generated. Garbage cans that are not kept in a cabinet often have a convertible lid that prevents an unpleasant odor from emerging. These lids can be problematic, however, if they require the client to frequently open and close the trashcan with dirty hands. It is a better option to have a garbage can with a lid that can be opened with a foot pedal.

Handling recycling

Most clients live in areas where recycling is mandatory. Even if it is not required, it is a good environmental practice to separate used cans, newspapers, plastic containers, and empty bottles. These items need to be washed before they are recycled, and the kitchen should have some sort of container where they can accumulate until they are brought to the curb. Most clients like to keep their recycling container next to the trashcan for convenience. If the newspapers need to be bundled, then the client should keep a pair of scissors and a roll of twine nearby. Recycling should be kept in a covered container; many companies sell attractive wooden, plastic, and metal recycling bins. The organizer could even paint the recycling bin to match the rest of the client's kitchen.

Organizing recipes

Clients who like to cook will probably amass a large number of recipes. It is important for these recipes to be organized in such a way that the client can access and use them easily. If the client uses a certain recipe very frequently, it could be taped to the inside of the cabinet door. Recipes can also be laminated so that they do not become spattered with grease or oil. Clients who like to clip recipes out of magazines should obtain an index box with a set of tabbed dividers. The dividers can then be labeled for different food categories, like salads, desserts, and entrées. Some clients have success using a photo album or scrapbook for storing recipes. These books already have laminated pages that make it easy to keep recipes in good condition. A still more advanced way to deal with piles of recipe clippings is to compile a recipe database so that the client can instantly access any of his or her favorites on a laptop or smartphone.

Storing china

Many clients will have sets of fine china that they highly value but rarely use. When the client almost never uses his or her fine china, it may be stored at a considerable distance from the dining room. However, many clients like to keep their china on display. If the china set is large, it may make sense for the client to display some of the items in a cabinet and store the rest in the attic or basement. Sometimes, the client will be satisfied with just displaying a few of the more esoteric elements of the collection, like the butter tray or the gravy boat. China should always be stored with an eye towards its preservation. Newspaper or cloth should be inserted between each plate, dish, and bowl to prevent chipping.

Improvising a bar in the dining room

Clients may not have a separate bar, but they can organize their drinks area by placing all of the relevant materials in the same place. For instance, a client might place a slender armoire in the dining room where glasses, bowls, mixing equipment, and liquor bottles can be kept.

Clients who like to keep a more elaborate bar could obtain a deeper piece of furniture. Sometimes, an organizer will recommend that a client purchase a rolling cart to use as a bar: the client can simply move the cart to the place where company is being entertained. This arrangement is especially good for clients who spend a great deal of time near a pool or on an outdoor patio.

Storing miscellaneous items in the dining room

Many clients fill valuable dining room storage space with items that are used only infrequently. For instance, clients often have a collection of party materials, like special napkins, streamers, and candles. If these items are only used a few times a year, it is not necessary to store them in the dining room. Instead, the client may want to place these items in a box in the attic or basement. Another item that clients often have in abundance is candles. If the client does not use candles very often in the dining room, then he or she only needs to keep a few on hand. Matches and candlesticks should be kept in the same place as spare candles. Clients should be reminded that candles are extremely inexpensive, so it is not necessary to save those that have already been burned to stumps.

Ways a family room can be divided into zones

One way to begin organizing a family room is to divide it into zones according to function. For instance, there may be separate areas of the family room for watching television, reading, conversing, or playing music. There might be a special area of the family room where people gather together to play cards or board games. Once the room has been divided into different zones, it becomes easier to identify where items should be stored. As in other areas of the house, the best policy is to store items close to their site of use. The organizer should also consider whether any of the activities that are performed in the family room interfere with one another. For instance, it can be difficult for people to read while others are watching television. It would not make sense, then, to place a quiet reading nook in the same area as the entertainment center.

Organizing entertainment equipment

Electronic equipment is continually getting smaller and more efficient, but it can still occupy a great deal of space in a client's family room. One way to resolve this issue is to mount the television on a wall bracket. This is especially successful when the client has a flat-screen television. Another way to make the television less obtrusive is to place it inside a wardrobe or armoire. Indeed, some clients place all of their entertainment equipment inside a piece of furniture with doors so that it is out of view when not in use. A tall wardrobe will typically have a set of drawers that can be used to store CDs, DVDs, and other related items. Whenever possible, the client should obtain a universal remote control that will operate all of their entertainment equipment. Then all of the original remotes can be stored elsewhere. There should be a designated place for storing the universal remote control when it is not being used. The best place to store the remote control is next to the seat that is most often filled in the family room.

It is unsightly and even dangerous to have a mass of power cords running from the back of electronic equipment to the wall. As much as possible, the professional organizer should hide these cords. There are special cord bundlers that can be used to lasso thick tangles of wires. In particularly complicated networks, it may be useful to affix small labels. A professional organizer will want to place pieces of furniture in front of all electrical outlets that are being used. The organizer can then obtain an extension cord with a flat head that allows the furniture to be pushed flush against the wall. The arrangement of furniture in the room should leave at least one accessible electrical socket.

Organizing artwork and wall hangings

When a client has an excessive amount of artwork and photographs on his or her walls, it can create a cluttered appearance that sets the tone for the rest of the space. An organizer will usually ask the client to isolate his or her most important pieces of art and take the rest down. Also, there is nothing wrong with rotating the artwork displayed in the house. This can give the client a fresh look at items with which he or she may have become bored. If surfaces are cluttered with framed photographs, the client may want to consider hanging them on the wall. Before hanging the artwork, the organizer and client may want to tape a piece of poster board roughly the same size as the frame to get an idea of how the artwork will fill the wall space.

Organizing books

Clients who love to read may amass too many books. A home library can be a wonderful thing, but the organizer needs to help the client get it into some kind of working order. Books do not need to be arranged in a rigid structure, but it is generally a good idea to group them together by category or author. Any book that the client has already read and does not plan to read again, or which the client could easily obtain at a local library, should be discarded. If the client cannot bear to part with his or her books but there is not enough shelf space to accommodate all of them, the excess books can be placed in boxes and put in

- 71 -

storage. Then, in the future, the client can place these books on the shelves and place some others in storage.

Creating extra storage space in the family room

In many family rooms, the client will have a traditional set of end and coffee tables that are handsome, but which occupy a great deal of space without adding much room for storage. Instead of end tables, the client might use small chests or cabinets. If the client wants to keep his or her end tables, the organizer could suggest placing some wicker baskets underneath them. In lieu of a coffee table, the client might consider a trunk. Similarly, a client might substitute a small trunk outfitted with a cushion on top instead of an ottoman. Organizers can even create shallow containers that slide under sofas and easy chairs. These can be great places to store magazines, throw blankets, and television programming guides.

How parents can encourage their children to keep the playroom organized

Keeping a playroom organized can be a frustrating task, but there are a few simple steps a professional can recommend to ease this process. For one thing, the organizer could help the client create a set of color-coordinated containers. These containers can be used to hold different types of toys, like blocks, stuffed animals, or dolls. The parent can then make it a rule that the child must put away all of his or her toys in the appropriate bin before leaving the playroom. Parents should also be ruthless about discarding games and play equipment with broken or lost parts. The same is true for toys and dolls the child no longer uses. Parents can teach their children a great lesson about generosity by encouraging him or her to donate unused items to charity.

Organizing puzzles, games, and crafts supplies in the playroom

The boxes for puzzles and board games tend to collapse and fall apart, allowing tiny pieces to scatter about the playroom. One solution to this problem is to move all of the puzzle and board game pieces to large Ziploc bags where they are more likely to stay together. All of the boards associated with the games can be lined along the side of the shelf. Another common source of clutter in the playroom is arts and crafts supplies. One way to begin organizing these objects is to group them by activity. For instance, all of the painting supplies can be placed together, as well as all of the crayons and markers. Whenever possible, an organizer should obtain shallow bins for the playroom. Children may have a hard time reaching all the way into a deep bin, and are less likely to move other objects out of the way to see what is at the bottom. Also, if children are not yet old enough to read, storage bins should be labeled with pictures rather than words.

Managing clothes

When embarking on a bedroom organization project, typically one of the first steps is to sort through the client's clothes. As with other sorting projects, the first step is to take all of the clothes out of the closet, dresser, and other storage areas and lay them on the floor or bed. The client should then group all of the like clothing items together. At this point, it will be possible for the client to identify items that he or she no longer needs or wants. If the client has several versions of a clothing item that will only be used occasionally, he or she should consider discarding some. For instance, female clients typically do not need three or four "little black dresses." Clients who insist on keeping a large number of clothes should consider creating a catalog for organizing them. This is done by photographing all of the clothes and then storing the images either on a computer or in an album. Then, the client can refer to the catalog and make wardrobe choices without having to dig through his or her closet or dresser.

Alternatives to storing clothing in a dresser

Many people assume that clothes have to be stored in a dresser, but there are other ways to resolve the storage issue. Indeed, when dressers are overfilled, the clothes inside tend to get wrinkled, and it is difficult to see everything that is inside the drawer. If possible, an organizer might recommend that clients stack all of their clothing items on a set of shelves, whether in the bedroom or in an adjacent closet. Another place to store clothes is under the bed. Organizers can obtain a set of handsome wooden or metal storage bins that easily slide out. Another problem with dressers is that they tend to be outfitted with mirrors that only give an image of the person's top half. A better option is to place a full-length mirror on the back of a bedroom or closet door. When the dresser is no longer needed in the bedroom, it can be used somewhere else in the house.

Organizing a nightstand

The nightstand, or bedside table, is frequently the site of paper clutter. Also, many clients accumulate little bottles of lotion, cotton swabs, and tissues in this area. The professional organizer should always recommend that clients refrain from keeping business or financial paperwork on or near the bedside table. It is not very relaxing to have a stack of utility bills on the nightstand. Cleaning the nightstand can be made easier by placing all of the items on it on a single tray which can then be lifted so that the surface of the table can be wiped clean. The organizer should also encourage the client to keep only a couple of books or magazines by the bedside. The books and magazines that a client is intending to read should be kept elsewhere. Unread books and magazines can be a hidden source of stress and anxiety for many clients.

Organizing purses

For many clients, an overstuffed and jumbled purse is just a microcosm of their disorganized lives. Clients need to learn a few basic strategies for handling chronic clutter in their purse or wallet. For one thing, clients should get in the habit of cleaning out their purse at least every week. Many clients amass big collections of business cards which occupy far too much space. The client should get used to placing all of the information from business cards into a notebook or online database. Eventually, the client will actually save time by regularly transferring all of this information rather than having to sort through a stack of cards to find a particular phone number. The client should also consider how often he or she actually uses the things in his or her purse. Clients may have a stack of credit and membership cards, few of which ever come out of the purse. The client should consider which of these are the most essential and discard the rest.

Organizing makeup

One common source of clutter in the bathroom is makeup. Many clients accumulate dozens of different shades of mascara, lipstick, blush, and other cosmetic products. It is easy for these to become jumbled. One way to approach this problem is to separate groups of makeup by use. For instance, many clients use a different set of cosmetic products during the day than they do at night.

These two sets of products can be grouped separately. Also, clients should get in the habit of setting aside all of the sample sizes of makeup they have collected. When necessary, clients should group the sample containers by category and place them in individual baskets. Also, clients should be aware that makeup products can expire and should discard any items that have outlived their usefulness.

Organizing a medicine cabinet

Clients will be able to get the most use from their medicine cabinet when it is not full of bottles and beauty equipment. Only the essential items that are used frequently should be kept in the medicine cabinet, as for instance deodorant, toothpaste, and razors. As in other shelving units, the space in a medicine cabinet can be increased by mounting small brackets underneath each shelf. For instance, there are small wire racks that can be used to hold a toothbrush or straight razor. If the client does not have a medicine cabinet, the organizer may improvise one with a wire rack mounted on the wall. When the wall is made of tiles, the organizer can affix a rack to it with suction cups. Even if the client does have a medicine cabinet, it can be useful to create extra storage with a hanging basket or rack.

Organizing the shower or bathtub

Clients who have children will often find their tub cluttered with toys. This problem can be resolved by affixing a small open container to the shower rod or the wall next to the bathtub. Children do not need more than a few toys when they are in the tub. Bottles of shampoo and conditioner can be tidied by hanging a wire rack from the showerhead. Often, these racks will also include a small shelf for soap. There may also be a set of hooks from which the client can hang

washcloths and loofahs. The client will want to position the soap tray so that it is not likely to be continuously sprayed by water when the shower is on. Water allowed to run over the soap constantly diminishes its longevity and produces soap scum on the walls of the shower.

Organizing a laundry room

One easy way to begin the process of organizing a laundry room is to add a wardrobe or armoire. A laundry sorter can be placed at the bottom of this piece of furniture for dirty laundry to be separated. The shelf of the armoire can be used to store bottles of detergent and bleach. The insides of the doors of an armoire typically have hooks where towels and a lint roller can be kept. Finally, the top shelf is a good place to store a sewing kit and other miscellaneous items. If possible, the organizer should find a space near the dryer to keep a few clothes hangers. Some clothes will quickly become wrinkled if they are not immediately hung. The client will also need a table that can be devoted to folding laundry. If there is not enough room for a permanent table, then the organizer might improvise a folding table or a table that leans down from the wall. Clients should also limit the clothing that gets folded; it is not necessary, for instance, to fold underwear.

Sorting laundry

There are a few easy steps that clients can take to minimize the amount of work that needs to be done with laundry. To begin with, the members of the family should get in the habit of placing their dirty clothes in the hamper turned right side out with the pockets empty and the buttons buttoned. This will reduce the amount of time spent folding and putting away clothes after they have been dried. An even more advanced solution is to create and use a laundry sorter that divides dirty clothing into whites, lights, and darks. A typical laundry sorter has enough space in each section to hold multiple loads of laundry. When the client goes to do his or her laundry, all he or she needs to do is reach in and grab the contents of one container, instead of sorting all of the laundry by hand. There should also be a container near the dryer for unmatched socks. If a sock remains in the unmatched container for more than a month, it should be discarded.

Why clients should keep objects near where they are used

The idea seems obvious: the best place to store an item is close to where it is used. However, beginning professional organizers will be astonished at the distances clients make themselves travel in the accomplishment of mundane tasks. One common example is a kitchen in which coffee mugs are on the other side of the room from the coffee pot. A client who has this arrangement probably spends hours of his or her year trudging across the kitchen, bleary-eyed in search of a mug. One of the easiest solutions a professional organizer can offer is moving objects closer to where they are used. In some cases, many objects will be used in roughly the same place. For instance, a client who partakes in a number of craft activities may have a massive amount of supplies and equipment, all of which are used on a particular table. In this case, the organizer should place the most important and frequently used items within reach of the table, and the other items progressively farther away in relation to their necessity. Clients will be amazed at the time they save by taking this simple step.

Shopping

For many professional organizers, the most fun part of any project is shopping for new products. However, a professional organizer should restrain the urge to go shopping until the project has been fully assessed and initiated. An experienced professional organizer knows that it is impossible to determine how a project will develop, and therefore it is impossible to know exactly what organization products will be appropriate. It is rare that a professional can guess at the beginning of the project what he or she will need several hours or days later. Moreover, the interconnectedness of organization projects often reveals new areas that need to be managed, and therefore new products that need to be purchased. For all of these reasons, a professional organizer should show some restraint before going to the store. Instead, it is a good idea to use temporary storage at first so that both the organizer and the client can assess how products work in reality.

Issues to consider when shopping for products

For a professional organizer, any trip to the store is a research expedition. The organizer should not just be looking for new products and special deals, however. There are certain technical aspects of shopping for organization products that a professional must keep in mind. For instance, a professional organizer should always try to find similar products at different prices. Some clients will want to splurge on top-quality items, while others will be comfortable with purchasing low-cost goods. Naturally, a professional organizer also wants to discover value or places where good quality can be obtained for a relatively low price. The professional organizer needs to identify the protocols for making purchases at different stores: for instance, the organizer should determine how returns are handled and whether ordering products through the mail incurs large shipping and handling fees. The organizer should also know how long it will take to obtain any products that are delivered through the mail.

Online shopping

For a professional organizer, online shopping is the most convenient way to research and obtain products. The only real problem with online shopping is that it can present an excessive number of choices, which can make it difficult for the organizer to choose the right product. However, once a professional organizer becomes adept at navigating the most popular online retail sites, he or she will be able to present clients with a wealth of options. In many cases, the organizer will not have to pay sales tax on these purchases either. The professional organizer does need to investigate the size of shipping and handling charges associated with online purchases. As more and more business moves online, a professional organizer needs to learn how to negotiate this retail space. Most online retailers have excellent return policies, so the organizer should not be concerned about the cost of mailing an unwanted or faulty product back to the manufacturer. The only real problem with purchasing goods online is that it can take a few days for them to arrive, and clients can be impatient.

Catalog shopping

Many professional organizers love leafing through catalogs in search of new and inexpensive organization products. For those organizers who are not totally comfortable on the Internet, catalog shopping is a great way to survey a large number of products at once. One potential problem with catalog shopping is that purchases tend to be accompanied by high taxes and shipping and handling charges. Also, it is very important to research the return policy of the retailer fully before making a purchase. A more pressing problem with catalog shopping is that it can result in an accumulation of paper in the professional organizer's office. The organizer should practice the same paper management skills he or she preaches to clients: each catalog should be discarded as soon as the new edition arrives to succeed it. These days, most professional organizers feel that the clutter and hassle of dealing with catalogs outweighs their readability. Still, there are a few specialty retailers who primarily sell their goods through catalogs.

Shopping in stores

There are all sorts of different ways for professional organizers to obtain products, but many still prefer to purchase their goods in person at a local store. Professional organizers quickly learn the layouts of the supply and discount stores in their area so they can minimize their shopping time once a project is underway. There are obvious advantages to shopping in stores: products can be handled and assessed by eye, there will not be any delivery charges associated with the purchase, and returns are usually easy. Of course, it is much less time-consuming to browse retail websites than it is to visit several different stores. For this reason, a professional organizer should acquire a familiarity with the inventory of major relevant retailers before beginning operations. The professional organizer should also do some research on the house brands of various big-box retailers to determine the quality and durability of these products.

Major factors a to consider when evaluating products

It is tempting for a professional organizer to be enticed by new and innovative products, but professionals should remain focused on several key factors when evaluating options for their clients. For instance, a professional organizer should be attuned to the ease with which the products can be used. Clients with habitual organization problems cannot be depended upon to use a product that is challenging or labor-intensive. The organizer should also consider whether the product will be durable enough to endure repeated uses, should they be necessary. For instance, if the client manages a great deal of paperwork, his or her file folders should be able to endure frequent use. Organizers should be wary of products that have a number of different uses or parts. A client will be learning to use an entirely new organization system, and should not be called upon to also learn how to operate confusing new products. Finally, and most importantly, a professional organizer should ask himself whether the product will simplify or complicate the client's life. This question must be resolved satisfactorily before any purchase is made.

Considering style when selecting products for clients

For a professional organizer, the most important characteristic of a product is its function. Still, clients will want to have products that look nice. The design and aesthetics of a product are more important in some cases than others: for instance, storage bins that are to be kept in the basement do not need to be particularly handsome. However, a client will want to have attractive file folders and bins for his or her office. The organizer must always consider design from the perspective of the client; that is, he or she should purchase products that are aligned with the client's pre-existing or desired style. When a client has clear style preferences, the organizer should discuss purchases ahead of time. A professional organizer needs to be able to present each client with a variety of options for each product type. In some cases, the client will need to take some time to define his or her style before making selections.

Value of shopping in the company of the client

Professional organizers are divided on the question of whether it is useful to shop in the company of clients. Some organizers feel that being accompanied by a client slows their work, while others believe that time is saved by avoiding unwise purchases. One middle path is to do some preliminary browsing with clients, but then make final purchases alone. At the very least, a professional organizer needs to get a clear sense of the client's personal style before making any final purchases. One advantage of shopping with the client is that he or she can pay for the products at the point of sale, rather than reimbursing the organizer for them later. Also, the organizer might think of a new idea while shopping, and it can be useful to have the client there for feedback. Another possible strategy is to shop online at the client's house. This can be useful when a product needs to be purchased for a specific space because the organizer can check the listed measurements of the product.

Value of shopping independent of the client

In some cases, it is appropriate for a professional organizer to shop alone, without the client. This is especially true at the beginning of a project when an organizer might just be browsing to invigorate his or her creative imagination. In some cases, and particularly for a novice organizer, it will take a while to determine the right product for the client. An organizer might want to wander the aisles of a large retailer hoping that inspiration will strike. There is no reason for the client to come along on such an expedition. The organizer can always take a quick photo of any product in which he or she is interested and then confer with the client at their next meeting.

Value of a client shopping alone

On occasion, a professional organizer may request that a client do some shopping independently. There are some obvious advantages to this system: clients are sure to buy something they find attractive, and so there are likely to be fewer needs for returns. However, the client who is already overwhelmed by the scale of the organization project should not be asked to add shopping to his or her list of chores. The organizer should remember that clients have much less experience with and knowledge of organizing products, and so a description that seems self-evident to the professional may be mystifying to the client. When an organizer suggests that a client shop alone, the organizer should always give very specific instructions. In the best scenario, the organizer will give the client a specific list of products to purchase, as well as a list of possible sources, and then the client is free to shop around for the best value.

Billing clients for time spent shopping

Some professional organizers bill clients by the hour when they are shopping for them. This is appropriate when a shopping trip was undertaken for a single purpose and for a single client. When the client is being billed by the hour, the organizer needs to ensure that the shopping trip is as direct and quick as possible; he or she may not browse or research other products when on the clock. In most cases, it is a better idea to mark up the cost of the products given to the client. When a professional organizer shops alone, it is almost inevitable that he or she will want to look around at what's new or make purchases for multiple clients. Then, the organizer can simply add 30 to 40 percent to the cost of the items presented to the client. This may seem like a high markup, but an experienced professional organizer knows that he or she will spend a great deal of time shopping as well as returning unwanted products.

Obtaining a resale certificate

Whenever a professional organizer purchases a product and then sells it to the client with markup, he or she needs to obtain a resale certificate. These certificates are issued by the state and can usually be handled online. A resale certificate indicates that the business owner will obtain sales tax from the client. A professional organizer who resells products to clients must file a report with the state every quarter indicating the amount of money that is owed. Then, the organizer needs to make a quarterly payment. It is not a bad idea to discuss this protocol with a local accountant when beginning operations. In most states, however, the procedures are simple enough that an organizer with a little experience will be able to handle them alone.

Handling the assembly and installation of products

A professional organizer is not obliged to assemble and install the products he or she purchases for clients, but in most cases it is appropriate for him or her to do so. Some organization products may require technical skills beyond those of the organizer. For instance, in some cases a professional organizer will obtain large shelving units that must be assembled by a trained carpenter. A professional organizer should never undertake an assembly or installation project that requires power tools with which the organizer is unfamiliar. It is always better to sacrifice a little income in order to do the project correctly then it is to risk alienating a client whose new organization system falls apart weeks or months after it has been put in place. Professional organizers should try to make contacts within the construction and carpentry industries so that they will have reliable professionals to call upon when necessary.

Paper filing system

The most important qualities of a system for filing paper are clarity, simplicity, and accessibility. As a general rule, the client should be able to find and access any piece of paper in under a minute. Also, a filing system should be comprehensive, meaning that there must be a place for every type of paper that enters the client's life. Paper should always be stored where it is used, so business files should be kept next to the desk and magazines should be stored next to the sofa or armchair in which they are read. If the client deals with certain types of paperwork in multiple places, the professional organizer may encourage him or her to settle on one or place the paperwork close to the location used more often. A professional organizer should never create a system in which a client routinely has to get out of his or her chair and walk to find a particular document. Also, a professional organizer should never establish a system that allows miscellaneous bits of paper, like catalogs and bills, to accumulate on counters and desktops.

Esssential items
Before beginning to organize client paperwork, a professional organizer should have certain pieces of equipment on hand. For one thing, the organizer should have a good set of manila file folders. These may be the property of the client, or they may be temporary storage supplied by the organizer. Another important piece of equipment is the trashcan or recycle bin. If the project is a success, this receptacle will be filled and emptied several times over. Another important component of a paper filing project is a running account of how long certain types of documents need to be

kept on hand. One common reason for paper clutter is that the client doesn't want to throw away documents while they are relevant, but doesn't notice when the documents become irrelevant. Eventually, the client will have a large stack of forgotten and unnecessary paperwork. One foundation of an efficient paper filing system is a set of term limits for each type of paper. It is also a good idea to have a set of post-it notes on hand when filing paper so that the various stacks can be given provisional category names.

Initial steps in a paper sorting process
The home base of a paper sorting process should be either where the highest volume of clutter exists or where the client handles most of his or her paperwork. If these are not the same place, the client should consider moving his or her paperwork closer to its place of use. The first piles to tackle are those on visible surfaces. These files usually reveal the types of paperwork for which the client does not have a defined place. When the client does not know where a piece of paperwork goes, or cannot even identify it, it should be put in a box and set aside for later. As each piece of paperwork is processed, the professional organizer and client should identify it and decide whether it needs to be saved. In some cases, the client may need to evaluate exactly why he or she has a particular piece of paper in the first place. Paperwork is to be filed according to its intended use, so it is important to make this use explicit at the beginning of the filing process.

After a piece of paper has been identified, it should be placed in a manila file folder that has been labeled in pencil. The label does not have to be the final or permanent title for the file, but it must be something that will remind the client of what is inside. There is no sense in using formal or overly general titles if the client will not understand or remember them. Simplicity, precision, and brevity are the desired characteristics for these labels. As always, categories should be defined according to the desires and needs of the client, and not according to preconceived category structures of the organizer. The organizer should probably ask the client to confirm title selections before writing them on the file folders. An experienced professional organizer will discover that there are almost as many different appropriate labeling systems as there are individual clients.

How sorted paper should be organized

As paperwork is identified and sorted, file folders will begin to accumulate. Just as there are similarities between the pieces of paper in each file folder, there will be similarities between file folders. For instance, there may be different file folders related to auto repair, insurance, and fuel expenses. These file folders should be kept together. There will also probably be groups of personal and financial file folders. One easy way to distinguish groups of file folders is to use color coding. Manila file folders are all the same color, so the professional organizer can use colored stickers to indicate file category. As the files accumulate, they should be placed in containers together. Paperwork that is immediately actionable should be placed into a special file. This would include bills that need to be paid, invitations that need to be answered, and any other documents that require a swift response. At some point during the filing project, the client should plow through all of the pressing matters. The paperwork associated can then be fed into the developing file system.

Necessity of patience and persistence when sorting paperwork

Many clients will begin a paper sorting process with the best of intentions, only to become bogged down almost immediately. To avoid this, professional organizers should establish some strict rules. During the initial sort, the client should not read any papers or respond to any actionable paperwork. This sort of delay can be fatal to the momentum of a filing process. The intention of this initial sort is to rapidly gather documents in groups of affinity, not to handle every piece of paperwork that exists. It is the responsibility of the professional organizer to keep the client focused during this process. The professional organizer may need to be stern at times. However, the process can be eased by creating a list of tasks at the beginning and then reminding the client to restrict himself to the activities on this list. Some clients may need a long time to go through all of their paperwork. It may take some clients a while to get accustomed to the sorting process, and it is not the place of a professional organizer to prod the client too aggressively. However, the client should be reminded that there will be time to deal with each piece of paperwork in the future.

Final steps

After the client has placed all of his or her paperwork into file folders and grouped the folders by theme, it is time to transfer all the paperwork into a more permanent storage system. The client should acquire a set of multicolored folders so that the file folder categories already established can be maintained. It is a good idea to buy the best quality folders because cheaply made folders tend to disintegrate rather quickly. These folders should be given simple, easy-to-read labels. It is always best to have light-colored file folders and to label them with black ink. Some clients elect to use label makers, which can create a handsome and very legible file title. After the filing project is complete, the client may even want to take some additional steps to prevent future paper clutter. One prevention method is to unsubscribe from as many catalogs and automatic mailings as possible. There are some websites that offer a comprehensive "opt out" from junk mail.

Length of time various types of paper should be kept

One paper problem that many clients have is confusion over how long various types of paper need to be retained. For instance, many clients feel that it is important to keep a hard copy of each of their bank statements for several years. However, with the advent of online banking and bill paying services, there is much less necessity for this. Many banks allow clients to review the statements from the entire history of their account online. Of course, if the client feels uneasy about trusting the bank to maintain records, he or she can confirm the accuracy of the online statement and then save it as a file on his or her computer. Most bills, however, can be discarded after the conclusion of the accounting year. For instance, clients will never be called upon to produce their water bill from 18 months ago. For more specific advice about tax paperwork, clients and professional organizers should consult an accountant. The amount of time that medical records should be kept is also variable. If the information in the record could have some future utility for the client, it should be retained; otherwise, it may be discarded after the conclusion of the accounting year.

Auto records, appointment books, credit card statements, ATM slips, home improvement records, and household appraisal records
Clients are often scared to discard any piece of paperwork they feel may be useful in the future, but in many cases what seems essential is actually quite unnecessary. Records related to an automobile only need to be kept so long as the vehicle is owned. It may be necessary to keep some of these

documents until the conclusion of the tax year if the vehicle is sold or totaled. Retaining appointment books is at the discretion of the client; some people like to hang onto these as records of their past. Credit card statements, on the other hand, only need to be kept until the annual interest statement is issued by the credit card company. Statements related to tax purchases should be kept for six years. ATM slips only need to be retained until they are confirmed against the monthly bank statement. Home improvement records should be kept as long as the client owns that home. Inventory and appraisal records related to the household should only be kept as long as they are relevant. Many homeowners choose to update these records every year.

Catalogs, magazines, dividend payment records, and health records
Catalogs become obsolete very quickly, and yet they are a huge source of clutter for many people. A catalog can be discarded as soon as the next edition arrives because the inventory and pricing of the dealer can change from one edition to the next. Magazines can be more difficult because clients often have articles they feel they will get around to reading. It is worth noting that most magazines have online archives where older articles can be found. Most professional organizers recommend that a magazine be discarded as soon as the new issue arrives, particularly if it is a magazine focused on current events or other timely information. It is recommended that clients keep their dividend payment records until they receive the annual statement. Sometimes, it is necessary to confirm the information in the annual statement against dividend records, and these documents may also be useful for the composition of tax forms. There is some dispute about the necessity of retaining health records. A good rule of thumb is to retain any document that

contains information that might be of use in the future. Also, clients should exercise caution before discarding health records more so than for almost any other document.

Insurance policies and investments
The recommended policy for retaining paperwork related to insurance policies depends on the type of insurance. The paperwork associated with automotive, homeowner's, and liability policies must be kept through the statute of limitations. This duration may vary by jurisdiction, and the professional organizer should be familiar with the statutes in his or her area. All of the paperwork associated with life, health, personal property, disability, or umbrella policies should be retained so long as the policy is active. It is unlikely that much of this paperwork will ever be required, but the potential cost of not having it is prohibitive. The client should maintain documents related to investment purchases as long as the investments are owned. As for investment sales, these records only need to be maintained for six years because they may be requested during an audit by the Internal Revenue Service.

Mortgage/loan discharge, pay stubs, property bills of purchase, and receipts
All the paperwork associated with the discharge of a mortgage or loan should be retained as long as the home is owned or at least six years after the discharge. The term of six years is indicated because this is the length of time within which the Internal Revenue Service may legally request documentation related to these issues. The client should keep his or her pay stubs until they have been verified by a W-2 statement. The W-2 is typically issued by January 31 of the succeeding year. All property bills of purchase should be kept as long as the property is owned. Indeed, this documentation should be kept in a safe place. Receipts should be kept for the entirety of the tax year, and

some clients may want to keep their receipts even longer than this. On this subject, it is best to consult an accountant.

Resumes, safe deposit boxes, taxes, utilities, vital records, and estate planning
It is not necessary to keep a copy of an old resume on hand once it has become obsolete, though some clients choose to do so. The key to a safe deposit box, along with a record of its inventory, should be retained so long as the box is owned by the client. Many clients are confused about how long they need to keep their tax records. Though clients should always check with their accountant, the general rule is that tax records must be maintained for the current year as well as the six years prior. Records within this range may be requested by the Internal Revenue Service during an audit. Utility bills, on the other hand, only need to be kept until they've been paid unless the client will try to deduct this expense from his or her taxes. All vital records, like birth certificates, marriage certificates, and death certificates, should be retained forever. The same is true of all documents related to estate planning, like wills and trusts.

Important paperwork that could be placed in a safe deposit box

Paperwork may seem like an indestructible force to the client with the cluttered home, but it is actually quite fragile, so the professional organizer should encourage the client to store his or her most important documents in a safe deposit box. For instance, a client may want to store the title to his automobile in a safe deposit box. This is also a good place to put vital information, like birth certificates, adoption papers, death certificates, marriage certificates, and divorce decrees. Veterans often elect to put their military discharge papers in a safe deposit box. Other people put documents related to estate planning, like wills and trusts, in a safe place. Immigrants may want to put their citizenship papers in a safe deposit box, and clients who travel abroad may want to store their passports there. Finally, clients may want to place any documentation related to life insurance policies, copyrights, or patents in a safe deposit box.

Evaluation, Follow-up, and Maintenance

Evaluation phase of an organization project

After an organization plan is implemented, the organizer and client need to take a step back and evaluate its success. To an extent, this process will be occurring throughout the project. If the client has misgivings about the plan, for instance, he or she should confer with the organizer to evaluate it. All of this sort of feedback should be handled immediately, but it will also be necessary to hold a formal evaluation meeting after the plan is fully implemented. When changes are required, the organizer should make them and then allow a little time to see their effects. Part of the evaluation process is teaching clients how to maintain their organization system. A professional organizer should never just complete his or her work and then head for the door. He or she must always indicate to the client that the lines of communication will remain open so long as the client desires. In many cases, professional organizers develop long-term relationships with clients, helping them adjust and evolve their organization systems as their lives change.

Necessity of constant maintenance after the implementation phase of an organization project

Even the most ingenious and practical organization solutions will ultimately fail if the client does not commit to regular maintenance. The mark of a great solution, however, is that it minimizes the amount of required maintenance. A good rule of thumb is that the client should have to spend no more than a few minutes every day restoring the physical space to its optimal conditions. This does not mean that the client will spend no more than five minutes washing dishes in his or her new kitchen, but rather that reestablishing the best conditions in which to work should not take very long. Clients should never feel that the creation of an organization system has simply produced another chore. Instead, it should always be apparent that a small amount of effort maintaining the system will save the client a huge amount of time and energy over time. This should be self-evident in the system, but it is also the responsibility of the organizer to describe his or her work in such a way that it will be consistently appreciated by the client.

How to address backsliding by clients

It can be very frustrating for a professional organizer to work hard with the client on a project only to see the client revert to bad habits in between meetings. Backsliding is inevitable, however, especially when the client's organization problems are rooted in emotional or mental issues. One of the best ways to combat backsliding is to schedule work sessions close together. If a medium-sized project is scheduled to occur over several months, it will be virtually impossible for the client to develop good habits and keep the new organization system in place. When there are long gaps between meetings, the organizer needs to give the client a concrete list of expectations for the interval. An organizer should expect that the client will backslide at least a little until the new system is in place. However, the organizer should take whatever steps are necessary to minimize the consequences of backsliding. That is, the organizer should focus on work which, once done, will not need to be done again.

Strategies for maintaining paper and computer organization

Even after successfully purging their home or office of unnecessary paper, many clients have difficulty maintaining their progress. One problem is that clients may overestimate the amount of time they have for reading, and may continue to collect too many books and magazines. A possible solution to this problem is to keep a reading journal for several weeks and then use it as an indication of how much reading is possible. Another way to manage paperwork is to obtain a scanner that converts documents into digital images. Clients can manage their mail better by immediately paying and filing bills (or by using online bill-paying services) and by discarding junk mail as soon as it arrives in the mailbox. Clients should also discard any computer equipment that is no longer used. Technology is constantly advancing, so there is little hope that a device currently unused will ever become essential.

Maintaining clothes organization

To maintain the organization of their clothes, clients should get in the habit of immediately discarding any items that no longer fit or that have permanent stains. Clients should learn to be ruthless about getting rid of unwanted or ill-fitting clothes. If the client does not like the way a piece of clothing looks now, there is no reason to suspect that he or she will change his or her mind in the future. Clients can also get in the habit of running the washing machine and dryer when they are out of the house. Most modern appliances have safety features that prevent overflows and other malfunctions, so the client does not need to be present while the machine operates. Also, clients should learn to fold and put away their laundry as soon as it comes out of the dryer. Not only does this reduce clutter and the anxiety caused by unfinished tasks, but it also prevents wrinkles.

Shopping strategies that help maintain organization

Clients can adopt some shopping habits that will help them maintain their organization. For instance, clients should give themselves plenty of time when they shop. Oddly, people tend to make more unnecessary and thoughtless purchases when they feel rushed. If a client feels pressured to get out of the store quickly, he or she may not fully consider whether a potential purchase is necessary. Another shopping strategy is to always carry a list and only buy the items on it and nothing else. Clients should avoid letting themselves be led astray by bargains and tempting items. Finally, clients can reduce plastic and paper bag clutter by purchasing reusable canvas bags for their shopping. Eventually, the time saved by eschewing store bags will more than compensate the small expense of a more durable bag

Secret Key #1 - Time is Your Greatest Enemy

Pace Yourself

Wear a watch. At the beginning of the test, check the time (or start a chronometer on your watch to count the minutes), and check the time after every few questions to make sure you are "on schedule."

If you are forced to speed up, do it efficiently. Usually one or more answer choices can be eliminated without too much difficulty. Above all, don't panic. Don't speed up and just begin guessing at random choices. By pacing yourself, and continually monitoring your progress against your watch, you will always know exactly how far ahead or behind you are with your available time. If you find that you are one minute behind on the test, don't skip one question without spending any time on it, just to catch back up. Take 15 fewer seconds on the next four questions, and after four questions you'll have caught back up. Once you catch back up, you can continue working each problem at your normal pace.

Furthermore, don't dwell on the problems that you were rushed on. If a problem was taking up too much time and you made a hurried guess, it must be difficult. The difficult questions are the ones you are most likely to miss anyway, so it isn't a big loss. It is better to end with more time than you need than to run out of time.

Lastly, sometimes it is beneficial to slow down if you are constantly getting ahead of time. You are always more likely to catch a careless mistake by working more slowly than quickly, and among very high-scoring test takers (those who are likely to have lots of time left over), careless errors affect the score more than mastery of material.

Secret Key #2 - Guessing is not Guesswork

You probably know that guessing is a good idea. Unlike other standardized tests, there is no penalty for getting a wrong answer. Even if you have no idea about a question, you still have a 20-25% chance of getting it right.

Most test takers do not understand the impact that proper guessing can have on their score. Unless you score extremely high, guessing will significantly contribute to your final score.

Monkeys Take the Test

What most test takers don't realize is that to insure that 20-25% chance, you have to guess randomly. If you put 20 monkeys in a room to take this test, assuming they answered once per question and behaved themselves, on average they would get 20-25% of the questions correct. Put 20 test takers in the room, and the average will be much lower among guessed questions. Why?

1. The test writers intentionally write deceptive answer choices that "look" right. A

test taker has no idea about a question, so he picks the "best looking" answer, which is often wrong. The monkey has no idea what looks good and what doesn't, so it will consistently be right about 20-25% of the time.

2. Test takers will eliminate answer choices from the guessing pool based on a hunch or intuition. Simple but correct answers often get excluded, leaving a 0% chance of being correct. The monkey has no clue, and often gets lucky with the best choice.

This is why the process of elimination endorsed by most test courses is flawed and detrimental to your performance. Test takers don't guess; they make an ignorant stab in the dark that is usually worse than random.

$5 Challenge

Let me introduce one of the most valuable ideas of this course—the $5 challenge:

You only mark your "best guess" if you are willing to bet $5 on it.
You only eliminate choices from guessing if you are willing to bet $5 on it.

Why $5? Five dollars is an amount of money that is small yet not insignificant, and can really add up fast (20 questions could cost you $100). Likewise, each answer choice on one question of the test will have a small impact on your overall score, but it can really add up to a lot of points in the end.

The process of elimination IS valuable. The following shows your chance of guessing it right:

If you eliminate wrong answer choices until only this many remain:	Chance of getting it correct:
1	100%
2	50%
3	33%

However, if you accidentally eliminate the right answer or go on a hunch for an incorrect answer, your chances drop dramatically—to 0%. By guessing among all the answer choices, you are GUARANTEED to have a shot at the right answer.

That's why the $5 test is so valuable. If you give up the advantage and safety of a pure guess, it had better be worth the risk.

What we still haven't covered is how to be sure that whatever guess you make is truly random. Here's the easiest way:

Always pick the first answer choice among those remaining.

Such a technique means that you have decided, **before you see a single test question**, exactly how you are going to guess, and since the order of choices tells you nothing about which one is correct, this guessing technique is perfectly random.

This section is not meant to scare you away from making educated guesses or eliminating choices; you just need to define when a choice is worth eliminating. The $5 test, along with a pre-defined random guessing strategy, is the best way to make sure you reap all of the benefits of guessing.

Secret Key #3 - Practice Smarter, Not Harder

Many test takers delay the test preparation process because they dread the awful amounts of practice time they think necessary to succeed on the test. We have refined an effective method that will take you only a fraction of the time.

There are a number of "obstacles" in the path to success. Among these are answering questions, finishing in time, and mastering test-taking strategies. All must be executed on the day of the test at peak performance, or your score will suffer. The test is a mental marathon that has a large impact on your future.

Just like a marathon runner, it is important to work your way up to the full challenge. So first you just worry about questions, and then time, and finally strategy:

Success Strategy

1. Find a good source for practice tests.
2. If you are willing to make a larger time investment, consider using more than one study guide. Often the different approaches of multiple authors will help you "get" difficult concepts.
3. Take a practice test with no time constraints, with all study helps, "open book." Take your time with questions and focus on applying strategies.
4. Take a practice test with time constraints, with all guides, "open book."
5. Take a final practice test without open material and with time limits.

If you have time to take more practice tests, just repeat step 5. By gradually exposing yourself to the full rigors of the test environment, you will condition your mind to the stress of test day and maximize your success.

Secret Key #4 - Prepare, Don't Procrastinate

Let me state an obvious fact: if you take the test three times, you will probably get three different scores. This is due to the way you feel on test day, the level of preparedness you have, and the version of the test you see. Despite the test writers' claims to the contrary, some versions of the test WILL be easier for you than others.

Since your future depends so much on your score, you should maximize your chances of success. In order to maximize the likelihood of success, you've got to prepare in advance. This means taking practice tests and spending time learning the information and test taking strategies you will need to succeed.

Never go take the actual test as a "practice" test, expecting that you can just take it again if you need to. Take all the practice tests you can on your own, but when you go to take the official test, be prepared, be focused, and do your best the first time!

Secret Key #5 - Test Yourself

Everyone knows that time is money. There is no need to spend too much of your time or too little of your time preparing for the test. You should only spend as much of your precious time preparing as is necessary for you to get the score you need.

Once you have taken a practice test under real conditions of time constraints, then you will know if you are ready for the test or not.

If you have scored extremely high the first time that you take the practice test, then there is not much point in spending countless hours studying. You are already there.

Benchmark your abilities by retaking practice tests and seeing how much you have improved. Once you consistently score high enough to guarantee success, then you are ready.

If you have scored well below where you need, then knuckle down and begin studying in earnest. Check your improvement regularly through the use of practice tests under real conditions. Above all, don't worry, panic, or give up. The key is perseverance!

Then, when you go to take the test, remain confident and remember how well you did on the practice tests. If you can score high enough on a practice test, then you can do the same on the real thing.

General Strategies

The most important thing you can do is to ignore your fears and jump into the test immediately. Do not be overwhelmed by any strange-sounding terms. You have to jump into the test like jumping into a pool—all at once is the easiest way.

Make Predictions

As you read and understand the question, try to guess what the answer will be. Remember that several of the answer choices are wrong, and once you begin reading them, your mind will immediately become cluttered with answer choices designed to throw you off. Your mind is typically the most focused immediately after you have read the question and digested its contents. If you can, try to predict what the correct answer will be. You may be surprised at what you can predict.

Quickly scan the choices and see if your prediction is in the listed answer choices. If it is, then you can be quite confident that you have the right answer. It still won't hurt to check the other answer choices, but most of the time, you've got it!

Answer the Question

It may seem obvious to only pick answer choices that answer the question, but the test writers can create some excellent answer choices that are wrong. Don't pick an answer just because it sounds right, or you believe it to be true. It MUST answer the question. Once you've made your selection, always go back and check it against the question and make sure that you didn't misread the question and that the answer choice does answer the question posed.

Benchmark

After you read the first answer choice, decide if you think it sounds correct or not. If it doesn't, move on to the next answer choice. If it does, mentally mark that answer choice. This doesn't mean that you've definitely selected it as your answer choice, it just means that it's the best you've seen thus far. Go ahead and read the next choice. If the next choice is worse than the one you've already selected, keep going to the next answer choice. If the next choice is better than the choice you've already selected, mentally mark the new answer choice as your best guess.

The first answer choice that you select becomes your standard. Every other answer choice must be benchmarked against that standard. That choice is correct until proven otherwise by another answer choice beating it out. Once you've decided that no other answer choice seems as good, do one final check to ensure that your answer choice answers the question posed.

Valid Information

Don't discount any of the information provided in the question. Every piece of information may be necessary to determine the correct answer. None of the information in the question is there to throw you off (while the answer choices will certainly have information to throw you off). If two seemingly unrelated topics are discussed, don't ignore either. You can be confident there is a relationship, or it wouldn't be included in the question, and you are probably going to have to determine what is that relationship to find the answer.

Avoid "Fact Traps"

Don't get distracted by a choice that is factually true. Your search is for the answer that answers the question. Stay focused and don't fall for an answer that is true but irrelevant. Always go back to the question and make sure you're choosing an answer that actually answers the question and is not just a true statement. An answer can be factually correct, but it MUST answer the question asked. Additionally, two answers can both be seemingly correct, so be sure to read all of the answer choices, and make sure that you get the one that BEST answers the question.

Milk the Question

Some of the questions may throw you completely off. They might deal with a subject you have not been exposed to, or one that you haven't reviewed in years. While your lack of knowledge about the subject will be a hindrance, the question itself can give you many clues that will help you find the correct answer. Read the question carefully and look for clues. Watch particularly for adjectives and nouns describing difficult terms or words that you don't recognize. Regardless of whether you completely understand a word or not, replacing it with a synonym, either provided or one you more familiar with, may help you to understand what the questions are asking. Rather than wracking your mind about specific

- 90 -

detailed information concerning a difficult term or word, try to use mental substitutes that are easier to understand.

The Trap of Familiarity

Don't just choose a word because you recognize it. On difficult questions, you may not recognize a number of words in the answer choices. The test writers don't put "make-believe" words on the test, so don't think that just because you only recognize all the words in one answer choice that that answer choice must be correct. If you only recognize words in one answer choice, then focus on that one. Is it correct? Try your best to determine if it is correct. If it is, that's great. If not, eliminate it. Each word and answer choice you eliminate increases your chances of getting the question correct, even if you then have to guess among the unfamiliar choices.

Eliminate Answers

Eliminate choices as soon as you realize they are wrong. But be careful! Make sure you consider all of the possible answer choices. Just because one appears right, doesn't mean that the next one won't be even better! The test writers will usually put more than one good answer choice for every question, so read all of them. Don't worry if you are stuck between two that seem right. By getting down to just two remaining possible choices, your odds are now 50/50. Rather than wasting too much time, play the odds. You are guessing, but guessing wisely because you've been able to knock out some of the answer choices that you know are wrong. If you are eliminating choices and realize that the last answer choice you are left with is also obviously wrong, don't panic. Start over and consider each choice again. There may easily be something that you missed the first time and will realize on the second pass.

Tough Questions

If you are stumped on a problem or it appears too hard or too difficult, don't waste time. Move on! Remember though, if you can quickly check for obviously incorrect answer choices, your chances of guessing correctly are greatly improved. Before you completely give up, at least try to knock out a couple of possible answers. Eliminate what you can and then guess at the remaining answer choices before moving on.

Brainstorm

If you get stuck on a difficult question, spend a few seconds quickly brainstorming. Run through the complete list of possible answer choices. Look at each choice and ask yourself, "Could this answer the question satisfactorily?" Go through each answer choice and consider it independently of the others. By systematically going through all possibilities, you may find something that you would otherwise overlook. Remember though that when you get stuck, it's important to try to keep moving.

Read Carefully

Understand the problem. Read the question and answer choices carefully. Don't miss the question because you misread the terms. You have plenty of time to read each question thoroughly and make sure you understand what is being asked. Yet a happy medium must be attained, so don't waste too much time. You must read carefully, but efficiently.

Face Value

When in doubt, use common sense. Always accept the situation in the problem at face value. Don't read too much into it. These problems will not require you to make huge leaps of logic. The test writers aren't trying to throw you off with a cheap trick. If you have to go beyond creativity and make a leap of logic in order to have an answer choice answer the question, then you should look at the other answer choices. Don't overcomplicate the problem by creating theoretical relationships or explanations that will warp time or space. These are normal problems rooted in reality. It's just that the applicable relationship or explanation may not be readily apparent and you have to figure things out. Use your common sense to interpret anything that isn't clear.

Prefixes

If you're having trouble with a word in the question or answer choices, try dissecting it. Take advantage of every clue that the word might include. Prefixes and suffixes can be a huge help. Usually they allow you to determine a basic meaning. Pre- means before, post- means after, pro - is positive, de- is negative. From these prefixes and suffixes, you can get an idea of the general meaning of the word and try to put it into context. Beware though of any traps. Just because con- is the opposite of pro-, doesn't necessarily mean congress is the opposite of progress!

Hedge Phrases

Watch out for critical hedge phrases, led off with words such as "likely," "may," "can," "sometimes," "often," "almost," "mostly," "usually," "generally," "rarely," and "sometimes." Question writers insert these hedge phrases to cover every possibility. Often an answer choice will be wrong simply because it leaves no room for exception. Unless the situation calls for them, avoid answer choices that have definitive words like "exactly," and "always."

Switchback Words

Stay alert for "switchbacks." These are the words and phrases frequently used to alert you to shifts in thought. The most common switchback word is "but." Others include "although," "however," "nevertheless," "on the other hand," "even though," "while," "in spite of," "despite," and "regardless of."

New Information

Correct answer choices will rarely have completely new information included. Answer choices typically are straightforward reflections of the material asked about and will directly relate to the question. If a new piece of information is included in an answer choice that doesn't even seem to relate to the topic being asked about, then that answer choice is likely incorrect. All of the information needed to answer the question is usually provided for you in the question. You should not have to make guesses that are unsupported or choose answer choices that require unknown information that cannot be reasoned from what is given.

Time Management

On technical questions, don't get lost on the technical terms. Don't spend too much time on any one question. If you don't know what a term means, then odds are you aren't going to get much further since you don't have a dictionary. You should be able to immediately recognize whether or not you know a term. If you don't, work with the other clues that you have—the other answer choices and terms provided—but don't waste too much time trying to figure out a difficult term that you don't know.

Contextual Clues

Look for contextual clues. An answer can be right but not the correct answer. The contextual clues will help you find the answer that is most right and is correct. Understand the context in which a phrase or statement is made. This will help you make important distinctions.

Don't Panic

Panicking will not answer any questions for you; therefore, it isn't helpful. When you first see the question, if your mind goes blank, take a deep breath. Force yourself to mechanically go through the steps of solving the problem using the strategies you've learned.

Pace Yourself

Don't get clock fever. It's easy to be overwhelmed when you're looking at a page full of questions, your mind is full of random thoughts and feeling confused, and the clock is ticking down faster than you would like. Calm down and maintain the pace that you have set for yourself. As long as you are on track by monitoring your pace, you are guaranteed to have enough time for yourself. When you get to the last few minutes of the test, it may seem like you won't have enough time left, but if you only have as many questions as you should have left at that point, then you're right on track!

Answer Selection

The best way to pick an answer choice is to eliminate all of those that are wrong, until only one is left and confirm that is the correct answer. Sometimes though, an answer choice may immediately look right. Be careful! Take a second to make sure that the other choices are not equally obvious. Don't make a hasty mistake. There are only two times that you should stop before checking other answers. First is when you are positive that the answer choice you have selected is correct. Second is when time is almost out and you have to make a quick guess!

Check Your Work

Since you will probably not know every term listed and the answer to every question, it is important that you get credit for the ones that you do know. Don't miss any questions through careless mistakes. If at all possible, try to take a second to look back over your answer selection and make sure you've selected the correct answer choice and haven't made a costly careless mistake (such as marking an answer choice that you didn't mean to mark). The time it takes for this quick double check should more than pay for itself in caught mistakes.

Beware of Directly Quoted Answers

Sometimes an answer choice will repeat word for word a portion of the question or reference section. However, beware of such exact duplication. It may be a trap! More than likely, the correct choice will paraphrase or summarize a point, rather than being exactly the same wording.

Slang

Scientific sounding answers are better than slang ones. An answer choice that begins "To compare the outcomes..." is much more likely to be correct than one that begins "Because some people insisted..."

Extreme Statements

Avoid wild answers that throw out highly controversial ideas that are proclaimed as established fact. An answer choice that states the "process should used in certain situations, if..." is much more likely to be correct than one that states the "process should be discontinued completely." The first is a calm rational statement and doesn't even make a definitive, uncompromising stance, using a hedge word "if" to provide wiggle room, whereas the second choice is a radical idea and far more extreme.

Answer Choice Families

When you have two or more answer choices that are direct opposites or parallels, one of them is usually the correct answer. For instance, if one answer choice states "x increases" and another answer choice states "x decreases" or "y increases," then those two or three answer choices are very similar in construction and fall into the same family of answer choices. A family of answer choices consists of two or three answer choices, very similar in construction, but often with directly opposite meanings. Usually the correct answer choice will be in that family of answer choices. The "odd man out" or answer choice that doesn't seem to fit the parallel construction of the other answer choices is more likely to be incorrect.

Special Report: What Your Test Score Will Tell You About Your IQ

Did you know that most standardized tests correlate very strongly with IQ? In fact, your general intelligence is a better predictor of your success than any other factor, and most tests intentionally measure this trait to some degree to ensure that those selected by the test are truly qualified for the test's purposes.

Before we can delve into the relation between your test score and IQ, I will first have to explain what exactly is IQ. Here's the formula:

Your IQ = 100 + (Number of standard deviations below or above the average)*15

Now, let's define standard deviations by using an example. If we have 5 people with 5 different heights, then first we calculate the average. Let's say the average was 65 inches. The standard deviation is the "average distance" away from the average of each of the members. It is a direct measure of variability. If the 5 people included Jackie Chan and Shaquille O'Neal, obviously there's a lot more variability in that group than a group of 5 sisters who are all within 6 inches in height of each other. The standard deviation uses a number to characterize the average range of difference within a group.

A convenient feature of most groups is that they have a "normal" distribution. It makes sense that most things would be normal, right? Without getting into a bunch of statistical mumbo-jumbo, you just need to know that if you know the average of the group and the standard deviation, you can successfully predict someone's percentile rank in the group.

Confused? Let me give you an example. If instead of 5 people's heights, we had 100 people, we could figure out their rank in height JUST by knowing the average, standard deviation, and their height. We wouldn't need to know each person's height and manually rank them, we could just predict their rank based on three numbers.

What this means is that you can take your PERCENTILE rank that is often given with your test and relate this to your RELATIVE IQ of people taking the test - that is, your IQ relative to the people taking the test. Obviously, there's no way to know your actual IQ because the people taking a standardized test are usually not very good samples of the general population. Many of those with extremely low IQ's never achieve a level of success or competency necessary to complete a typical standardized test. In fact, professional psychologists who measure IQ actually have to use non-written tests that can fairly measure the IQ of those not able to complete a traditional test.

The bottom line is to not take your test score too seriously, but it is fun to compute your "relative IQ" among the people who took the test with you. I've done the calculations below. Just look up your percentile rank in the left and then you'll see your "relative IQ" for your test in the right hand column.

Percentile Rank	Your Relative IQ		Percentile Rank	Your Relative IQ
99	135		59	103
98	131		58	103
97	128		57	103
96	126		56	102
95	125		55	102
94	123		54	102
93	122		53	101
92	121		52	101
91	120		51	100
90	119		50	100
89	118		49	100
88	118		48	99
87	117		47	99
86	116		46	98
85	116		45	98
84	115		44	98
83	114		43	97
82	114		42	97
81	113		41	97
80	113		40	96
79	112		39	96
78	112		38	95
77	111		37	95
76	111		36	95
75	110		35	94
74	110		34	94
73	109		33	93
72	109		32	93
71	108		31	93
70	108		30	92
69	107		29	92
68	107		28	91
67	107		27	91
66	106		26	90
65	106		25	90
64	105		24	89
63	105		23	89
62	105		22	88
61	104		21	88
60	104		20	87

Special Report: What is Test Anxiety and How to Overcome It?

The very nature of tests caters to some level of anxiety, nervousness, or tension, just as we feel for any important event that occurs in our lives. A little bit of anxiety or nervousness can be a good thing. It helps us with motivation, and makes achievement just that much sweeter. However, too much anxiety can be a problem, especially if it hinders our ability to function and perform.

"Test anxiety," is the term that refers to the emotional reactions that some test-takers experience when faced with a test or exam. Having a fear of testing and exams is based upon a rational fear, since the test-taker's performance can shape the course of an academic career. Nevertheless, experiencing excessive fear of examinations will only interfere with the test-taker's ability to perform and chance to be successful.

There are a large variety of causes that can contribute to the development and sensation of test anxiety. These include, but are not limited to, lack of preparation and worrying about issues surrounding the test.

Lack of Preparation

Lack of preparation can be identified by the following behaviors or situations:

Not scheduling enough time to study, and therefore cramming the night before the test or exam
Managing time poorly, to create the sensation that there is not enough time to do everything
Failing to organize the text information in advance, so that the study material consists of the entire text and not simply the pertinent information
Poor overall studying habits

Worrying, on the other hand, can be related to both the test taker, or many other factors around him/her that will be affected by the results of the test. These include worrying about:

Previous performances on similar exams, or exams in general
How friends and other students are achieving
The negative consequences that will result from a poor grade or failure

There are three primary elements to test anxiety. Physical components, which involve the same typical bodily reactions as those to acute anxiety (to be discussed below). Emotional factors have to do with fear or panic. Mental or cognitive issues concerning attention spans and memory abilities.

Physical Signals

There are many different symptoms of test anxiety, and these are not limited to mental and emotional strain. Frequently there are a range of physical signals that will let a test taker know that he/she is suffering from test anxiety. These bodily changes can include the following:

Perspiring
Sweaty palms
Wet, trembling hands
Nausea
Dry mouth
A knot in the stomach
Headache
Faintness
Muscle tension
Aching shoulders, back and neck
Rapid heart beat
Feeling too hot/cold

To recognize the sensation of test anxiety, a test-taker should monitor him/herself for the following sensations:

The physical distress symptoms as listed above
Emotional sensitivity, expressing emotional feelings such as the need to cry or laugh too much, or a sensation of anger or helplessness
A decreased ability to think, causing the test-taker to blank out or have racing thoughts that are hard to organize or control.

Though most students will feel some level of anxiety when faced with a test or exam, the majority can cope with that anxiety and maintain it at a manageable level. However, those who cannot are faced with a very real and very serious condition, which can and should be controlled for the immeasurable benefit of this sufferer.

Naturally, these sensations lead to negative results for the testing experience. The most common effects of test anxiety have to do with nervousness and mental blocking.

Nervousness

Nervousness can appear in several different levels:

The test-taker's difficulty, or even inability to read and understand the questions on the test
The difficulty or inability to organize thoughts to a coherent form
The difficulty or inability to recall key words and concepts relating to the testing questions (especially essays)
The receipt of poor grades on a test, though the test material was well known by the test taker

Conversely, a person may also experience mental blocking, which involves:

Blanking out on test questions
Only remembering the correct answers to the questions when the test has already finished.

Fortunately for test anxiety sufferers, beating these feelings, to a large degree, has to do with proper preparation. When a test taker has a feeling of preparedness, then anxiety will be dramatically lessened.

The first step to resolving anxiety issues is to distinguish which of the two types of anxiety are being suffered. If the anxiety is a direct result of a lack of preparation, this should be considered a normal reaction, and the anxiety level (as opposed to the test results) shouldn't be anything to worry about. However, if, when adequately prepared, the test-taker still panics, blanks out, or seems to overreact, this is not a fully rational reaction. While this can be considered normal too, there are many ways to combat and overcome these effects.

Remember that anxiety cannot be entirely eliminated, however, there are ways to minimize it, to make the anxiety easier to manage. Preparation is one of the best ways to minimize test anxiety. Therefore the following techniques are wise in order to best fight off any anxiety that may want to build.

To begin with, try to avoid cramming before a test, whenever it is possible. By trying to memorize an entire term's worth of information in one day, you'll be shocking your system, and not giving yourself a very good chance to absorb the information. This is an easy path to anxiety, so for those who suffer from test anxiety, cramming should not even be considered an option.

Instead of cramming, work throughout the semester to combine all of the material which is presented throughout the semester, and work on it gradually as the course goes by, making sure to master the main concepts first, leaving minor details for a week or so before the test.

To study for the upcoming exam, be sure to pose questions that may be on the examination, to gauge the ability to answer them by integrating the ideas from your texts, notes and lectures, as well as any supplementary readings.

If it is truly impossible to cover all of the information that was covered in that particular term, concentrate on the most important portions, that can be covered very well. Learn these concepts as best as possible, so that when the test comes, a goal can be made to use these concepts as presentations of your knowledge.

In addition to study habits, changes in attitude are critical to beating a struggle with test anxiety. In fact, an improvement of the perspective over the entire test-taking experience can actually help a test taker to enjoy studying and therefore improve the overall experience. Be certain not to overemphasize the significance of the grade - know that the result of the test is neither a reflection of self worth, nor is it a measure of intelligence; one grade will not predict a person's future success.

To improve an overall testing outlook, the following steps should be tried:

Keeping in mind that the most reasonable expectation for taking a test is to expect to try to demonstrate as much of what you know as you possibly can.

Reminding ourselves that a test is only one test; this is not the only one, and there will be others.

The thought of thinking of oneself in an irrational, all-or-nothing term should be avoided at all costs.

A reward should be designated for after the test, so there's something to look forward to. Whether it be going to a movie, going out to eat, or simply visiting friends, schedule it in advance, and do it no matter what result is expected on the exam.

Test-takers should also keep in mind that the basics are some of the most important things, even beyond anti-anxiety techniques and studying. Never neglect the basic social, emotional and biological needs, in order to try to absorb information. In order to best achieve, these three factors must be held as just as important as the studying itself.

Study Steps

Remember the following important steps for studying:

Maintain healthy nutrition and exercise habits. Continue both your recreational activities and social pass times. These both contribute to your physical and emotional well being. Be certain to get a good amount of sleep, especially the night before the test, because when you're overtired you are not able to perform to the best of your best ability.

Keep the studying pace to a moderate level by taking breaks when they are needed, and varying the work whenever possible, to keep the mind fresh instead of getting bored. When enough studying has been done that all the material that can be learned has been learned, and the test taker is prepared for the test, stop studying and do something relaxing such as listening to music, watching a movie, or taking a warm bubble bath.

There are also many other techniques to minimize the uneasiness or apprehension that is experienced along with test anxiety before, during, or even after the examination. In fact, there are a great deal of things that can be done to stop anxiety from interfering with lifestyle and performance. Again, remember that anxiety will not be eliminated entirely, and it shouldn't be. Otherwise that "up" feeling for exams would not exist, and most of us depend on that sensation to perform better than usual. However, this anxiety has to be at a level that is manageable.

Of course, as we have just discussed, being prepared for the exam is half the battle right away. Attending all classes, finding out what knowledge will be expected on the exam, and knowing the exam schedules are easy steps to lowering anxiety. Keeping up with work will remove the need to cram, and efficient study habits will eliminate wasted time. Studying should be done in an ideal location for concentration, so that it is simple to become interested in the material and give it complete attention. A method such as SQ3R (Survey, Question, Read, Recite, Review) is a wonderful key to follow to make sure that the study habits are as effective as possible, especially in the case of learning from a textbook. Flashcards are great techniques for memorization. Learning to take good notes will mean that notes will be full of useful information, so that less sifting will need to be done to seek out what is pertinent for studying. Reviewing notes after class and then again on occasion will keep the information fresh in the mind. From notes that have been taken summary sheets and outlines can be made for simpler reviewing.

A study group can also be a very motivational and helpful place to study, as there will be a sharing of ideas, all of the minds can work together, to make sure that everyone understands, and the studying will be made more interesting because it will be a social occasion.

Basically, though, as long as the test-taker remains organized and self confident, with efficient study habits, less time will need to be spent studying, and higher grades will be achieved.

To become self confident, there are many useful steps. The first of these is "self talk." It has been shown through extensive research, that self-talk for students who suffer from test anxiety, should be well monitored, in order to make sure that it contributes to self confidence as opposed to sinking the student. Frequently the self talk of test-anxious students is negative or self-defeating, thinking that everyone else is smarter and faster, that they always mess up, and that if they don't do well, they'll fail the entire course. It is important to decreasing anxiety that awareness is made of self talk. Try writing any negative self thoughts and then disputing them with a positive statement instead. Begin self-encouragement as though it was a friend speaking. Repeat positive statements to help reprogram the mind to believing in successes instead of failures.

Helpful Techniques

Other extremely helpful techniques include:

Self-visualization of doing well and reaching goals
While aiming for an "A" level of understanding, don't try to "overprotect" by setting your expectations lower. This will only convince the mind to stop studying in order to meet the lower expectations.
Don't make comparisons with the results or habits of other students. These are individual factors, and different things work for different people, causing different results.
Strive to become an expert in learning what works well, and what can be done in order to improve. Consider collecting this data in a journal.
Create rewards for after studying instead of doing things before studying that will only turn into avoidance behaviors.
Make a practice of relaxing - by using methods such as progressive relaxation, self-hypnosis, guided imagery, etc - in order to make relaxation an automatic sensation.
Work on creating a state of relaxed concentration so that concentrating will take on the focus of the mind, so that none will be wasted on worrying.
Take good care of the physical self by eating well and getting enough sleep.
Plan in time for exercise and stick to this plan.

Beyond these techniques, there are other methods to be used before, during and after the test that will help the test-taker perform well in addition to overcoming anxiety.

Before the exam comes the academic preparation. This involves establishing a study schedule and beginning at least one week before the actual date of the test. By doing this, the anxiety of not having enough time to study for the test will be automatically eliminated. Moreover, this will make the studying a much more effective experience, ensuring that the learning will be an easier process. This relieves much undue pressure on the test-taker.

Summary sheets, note cards, and flash cards with the main concepts and examples of these main concepts should be prepared in advance of the actual studying time. A topic should never be eliminated from this process. By omitting a topic because it isn't expected to be on the test is only setting up the test-taker for anxiety should it actually appear on the exam. Utilize the course syllabus for laying out the topics that should be studied. Carefully go over the notes that were made in class, paying special attention to any of the issues that the professor took special care to emphasize while lecturing in class. In the textbooks, use the chapter review, or if possible, the chapter tests, to begin your review.

It may even be possible to ask the instructor what information will be covered on the exam, or what the format of the exam will be (for example, multiple choice, essay, free form, true-false). Additionally, see if it is possible to find out how many questions will be on the test. If a review sheet or sample test has been offered by the professor, make good use of it, above anything else, for the preparation for the test. Another great resource for getting to know the examination is reviewing tests from previous semesters. Use these tests to review, and aim to achieve a 100% score on each of the possible topics. With a few exceptions, the goal that you set for yourself is the highest one that you will reach.

Take all of the questions that were assigned as homework, and rework them to any other possible course material. The more problems reworked, the more skill and confidence will form as a result. When forming the solution to a problem, write out each of the steps. Don't simply do head work. By doing as many steps on paper as possible, much clarification and therefore confidence will be formed. Do this with as many homework problems as possible, before checking the answers. By checking the answer after each problem, a reinforcement will exist, that will not be on the exam. Study situations should be as exam-like as possible, to prime the test-taker's system for the experience. By waiting to check the answers at the end, a psychological advantage will be formed, to decrease the stress factor.

Another fantastic reason for not cramming is the avoidance of confusion in concepts, especially when it comes to mathematics. 8-10 hours of study will become one hundred percent more effective if it is spread out over a week or at least several days, instead of doing it all in one sitting. Recognize that the human brain requires time in order to assimilate new material, so frequent breaks and a span of study time over several days will be much more beneficial.

Additionally, don't study right up until the point of the exam. Studying should stop a minimum of one hour before the exam begins. This allows the brain to rest and put things in their proper order. This will also provide the time to become as relaxed as possible when going into the examination room. The test-taker will also have time to eat well and eat sensibly. Know that the brain needs food as much as the rest of the body. With enough food and enough sleep, as well as a relaxed attitude, the body and the mind are primed for success.

Avoid any anxious classmates who are talking about the exam. These students only spread anxiety, and are not worth sharing the anxious sentimentalities.

Before the test also involves creating a positive attitude, so mental preparation should also be a point of concentration. There are many keys to creating a positive attitude. Should fears become rushing in, make a visualization of taking the exam, doing well, and seeing an A written on the paper. Write out a list of affirmations that will bring a feeling of confidence, such as "I am doing well in my English class," "I studied well and know my material," "I enjoy this class." Even if the affirmations aren't believed at first, it sends a positive message to the subconscious which will result in an alteration of the overall belief system, which is the system that creates reality.

If a sensation of panic begins, work with the fear and imagine the very worst! Work through the entire scenario of not passing the test, failing the entire course, and dropping out of school, followed by not getting a job, and pushing a shopping cart through the dark alley where you'll live. This will place things into perspective! Then, practice deep breathing and create a visualization of the opposite situation - achieving an "A" on the exam, passing the entire course, receiving the degree at a graduation ceremony.

On the day of the test, there are many things to be done to ensure the best results, as well as the most calm outlook. The following stages are suggested in order to maximize test-taking potential:

Begin the examination day with a moderate breakfast, and avoid any coffee or beverages with caffeine if the test taker is prone to jitters. Even people who are used to managing caffeine can feel jittery or light-headed when it is taken on a test day.
Attempt to do something that is relaxing before the examination begins. As last minute cramming clouds the mastering of overall concepts, it is better to use this time to create a calming outlook.
Be certain to arrive at the test location well in advance, in order to provide time to select a location that is away from doors, windows and other distractions, as well as giving enough time to relax before the test begins.
Keep away from anxiety generating classmates who will upset the sensation of stability and relaxation that is being attempted before the exam.
Should the waiting period before the exam begins cause anxiety, create a self-distraction by reading a light magazine or something else that is relaxing and simple.

During the exam itself, read the entire exam from beginning to end, and find out how much time should be allotted to each individual problem. Once writing the exam, should more time be taken for a problem, it should be abandoned, in order to begin another problem. If there is time at the end, the unfinished problem can always be returned to and completed.

Read the instructions very carefully - twice - so that unpleasant surprises won't follow during or after the exam has ended.

When writing the exam, pretend that the situation is actually simply the completion of homework within a library, or at home. This will assist in forming a relaxed atmosphere, and will allow the brain extra focus for the complex thinking function.

Begin the exam with all of the questions with which the most confidence is felt. This will build the confidence level regarding the entire exam and will begin a quality momentum. This will also create encouragement for trying the problems where uncertainty resides.

Going with the "gut instinct" is always the way to go when solving a problem. Second guessing should be avoided at all costs. Have confidence in the ability to do well.

For essay questions, create an outline in advance that will keep the mind organized and make certain that all of the points are remembered. For multiple choice, read every answer, even if the correct one has been spotted - a better one may exist.

Continue at a pace that is reasonable and not rushed, in order to be able to work carefully. Provide enough time to go over the answers at the end, to check for small errors that can be corrected.

Should a feeling of panic begin, breathe deeply, and think of the feeling of the body releasing sand through its pores. Visualize a calm, peaceful place, and include all of the sights, sounds and sensations of this image. Continue the deep breathing, and take a few minutes to continue this with closed eyes. When all is well again, return to the test.

If a "blanking" occurs for a certain question, skip it and move on to the next question. There will be time to return to the other question later. Get everything done that can be done, first, to guarantee all the grades that can be compiled, and to build all of the confidence possible. Then return to the weaker questions to build the marks from there.

Remember, one's own reality can be created, so as long as the belief is there, success will follow. And remember: anxiety can happen later, right now, there's an exam to be written!

After the examination is complete, whether there is a feeling for a good grade or a bad grade, don't dwell on the exam, and be certain to follow through on the reward that was promised...and enjoy it! Don't dwell on any mistakes that have been made, as there is nothing that can be done at this point anyway.

Additionally, don't begin to study for the next test right away. Do something relaxing for a while, and let the mind relax and prepare itself to begin absorbing information again.

From the results of the exam - both the grade and the entire experience, be certain to learn from what has gone on. Perfect studying habits and work some more on confidence in order to make the next examination experience even better than the last one.

Learn to avoid places where openings occurred for laziness, procrastination and day dreaming.

Use the time between this exam and the next one to better learn to relax, even learning to relax on cue, so that any anxiety can be controlled during the next exam. Learn how to relax the body. Slouch in your chair if that helps. Tighten and then relax all of the different muscle groups, one group at a time, beginning with the feet and then working all the way up to the neck and face. This will ultimately relax the muscles more than they were to begin with. Learn how to breathe deeply and comfortably, and focus on this breathing going in and out as a relaxing thought. With every exhale, repeat the word "relax."

As common as test anxiety is, it is very possible to overcome it. Make yourself one of the test-takers who overcome this frustrating hindrance.

Special Report: Retaking the Test: What Are Your Chances at Improving Your Score?

After going through the experience of taking a major test, many test takers feel that once is enough. The test usually comes during a period of transition in the test taker's life, and taking the test is only one of a series of important events. With so many distractions and conflicting recommendations, it may be difficult for a test taker to rationally determine whether or not he should retake the test after viewing his scores.

The importance of the test usually only adds to the burden of the retake decision. However, don't be swayed by emotion. There a few simple questions that you can ask yourself to guide you as you try to determine whether a retake would improve your score:

1. What went wrong? Why wasn't your score what you expected?

Can you point to a single factor or problem that you feel caused the low score? Were you sick on test day? Was there an emotional upheaval in your life that caused a distraction? Were you late for the test or not able to use the full time allotment? If you can point to any of these specific, individual problems, then a retake should definitely be considered.

2. Is there enough time to improve?

Many problems that may show up in your score report may take a lot of time for improvement. A deficiency in a particular math skill may require weeks or months of tutoring and studying to improve. If you have enough time to improve an identified weakness, then a retake should definitely be considered.

3. How will additional scores be used? Will a score average, highest score, or most recent score be used?

Different test scores may be handled completely differently. If you've taken the test multiple times, sometimes your highest score is used, sometimes your average score is computed and used, and sometimes your most recent score is used. Make sure you understand what method will be used to evaluate your scores, and use that to help you determine whether a retake should be considered.

4. Are my practice test scores significantly higher than my actual test score?

If you have taken a lot of practice tests and are consistently scoring at a much higher level than your actual test score, then you should consider a retake. However, if you've taken five practice tests and only one of your scores was higher than your actual test score, or if your practice test scores were only slightly higher than your actual test score, then it is unlikely that you will significantly increase your score.

5. Do I need perfect scores or will I be able to live with this score? Will this score still allow me to follow my dreams?

What kind of score is acceptable to you? Is your current score "good enough?" Do you have to have a certain score in order to pursue the future of your dreams? If you won't be happy with your current score, and there's no way that you could live with it, then you should consider a retake. However, don't get your hopes up. If you are looking for significant improvement, that may or may not be possible. But if you won't be happy otherwise, it is at least worth the effort.

Remember that there are other considerations. To achieve your dream, it is likely that your grades may also be taken into account. A great test score is usually not the only thing necessary to succeed. Make sure that you aren't overemphasizing the importance of a high test score.

Furthermore, a retake does not always result in a higher score. Some test takers will score lower on a retake, rather than higher. One study shows that one-fourth of test takers will achieve a significant improvement in test score, while one-sixth of test takers will actually show a decrease. While this shows that most test takers will improve, the majority will only improve their scores a little and a retake may not be worth the test taker's effort.

Finally, if a test is taken only once and is considered in the added context of good grades on the part of a test taker, the person reviewing the grades and scores may be tempted to assume that the test taker just had a bad day while taking the test, and may discount the low test score in favor of the high grades. But if the test is retaken and the scores are approximately the same, then the validity of the low scores are only confirmed. Therefore, a retake could actually hurt a test taker by definitely bracketing a test taker's score ability to a limited range.

Special Report: Additional Bonus Material

Due to our efforts to try to keep this book to a manageable length, we've created a link that will give you access to all of your additional bonus material.

Please visit http://www.mometrix.com/bonus948/certproforg to access the information.